WHILE OTHERS SLEPT

First edition, published in 2001 by

WOODFIELD PUBLISHING
Woodfield House, Babsham Lane, Bognor Regis
West Sussex PO21 5EL, England.

ISBN 1-873203-72-1

While Others Slept

A first-hand account of the early
years of RAF Bomber Command

ERIC WOODS

Woodfield *Publishing*

BOGNOR REGIS · WEST SUSSEX · ENGLAND

Target map of Frankfurt

© copyright Her Britannic Majesty's Stationary Office.

Contents

Handley Page Hampden Mk 1.

'Chiefs of staff' crew (see chapter 15).

Introduction

It is a popular belief that, with the passage of time, memories fade and thus stories of dramatic wartime events from years long gone are now lost forever. To see the fallacy of this belief one only has to look at the popularity of Ex-Servicemen's Associations, and their regular reunions – the greatest of which is the annual march past of veterans and relatives at the Cenotaph in London – to appreciate that the bonding which took place between comrades in arms will remain in one form or another in perpetuity.

There has been a tendency for the media to highlight only a few key events of World War Two – such as the evacuation from Dunkirk, the battle of El Alamein and Fighter Command's great victory over the Luftwaffe in the Battle of Britain – these are, of course, highly significant events worthy of the attention, yet there were many other major contributions made elsewhere, which are seemingly now forgotten.

I decided to write about one of these overlooked contributions, one with which I am personally familiar, and of its undoubted role in smashing Nazi domination of Europe, namely that of Bomber Command of the Royal Air Force, a much-maligned force, whose valiant efforts, certain historians in recent years have attempted to denigrate.

In the dark days of 1940, with no British troops left in Europe and with Fighter Command struggling to hold the Luftwaffe at bay, Sir Winston Churchill had the wisdom to see that if the war was to be pursued to final victory, we had to take it *to* the "dreaded Hun" as soon as possible. The only means to achieve that objective at the time was via the efforts our then small bomber force, consisting of a motley array of twin-engined medium-range aircraft, poorly armed in many cases, and with built-in limitations brought about by a government desire to adhere to the requirements of the pre-war Geneva Agreement.

In these inadequate aircraft, young aircrews took to the skies and mounted attacks on strategic targets in Germany and occupied Europe with the intention of slowing the Nazi war machine by interrupting production and and transport. Initial attempts to mount daylight raids resulted in such heavy casualties that these were rapidly abandoned in favour of night-time operations only. Under cover of darkness, while others slept, the aircraft of the RAF went about their deadly business, facing stiff opposition from anti-aircraft batteries on the ground and Luftwaffe night-fighters in the air. Losses were very high, but this did not weaken the determination of the aircrews to take the war to the enemy. When you consider that these were very young men of about 20 years of age, their courage and fortitude seems all the more remarkable.

There is every reason to believe that without the repeated setbacks inflicted upon it by the efforts of Bomber Command, the Nazi war machine would have grown ever more powerful and eventually unstoppable.

I mentioned that Bomber Command was 'much maligned', which needs an explanation, hence my urge to highlight the bravery and fortitude of those early bomber crews with whom I served, and whose experiences form the substance of this story. This is not to underestimate the role of those who followed us, for without doubt, things got worse for bomber crews as the war progressed, for although our aircraft and tactics improved, so did the enemy's, and as pressure mounted to bring the war to a close, losses amongst Bomber Command aircrews reached devastating proportions.

But into our midst, in those early days, came the great Sir Arthur 'Butch' Harris who, with the approval of Sir Winston, and at a time when most of our cities were being destroyed by German bombing, determined a new strategic bombing policy, which progressively, and finally led to the 'saturation' bombing that has become such a contentious issue in the years since.

It is hard to understand why, in view of all that had preceded the introduction of this tactic, the brave aircrews of Bomber

Command became regarded by some in post-war years as villains. Criticism came to a head when raids on Nuremberg and Dresden were analysed by those who, in many instances, were not alive at the time and knew nothing about the pain and sacrifices of war.

Sad to say, even Sir Winston seemed then to deny approval of Sir Arthur's policy, in spite of his former support and knowledge of its tremendous contribution to ending the war. There is little doubt that this was a blow to Harris's faith and an insult to the memory of the many brave crews who died, as well as those who live on.

The climax of this backlash was the behaviour of the poor ill-informed folk who almost spoiled the ceremony when the Queen Mother unveiled the memorial to Sir Arthur, a memorial commissioned and paid for by the survivors of Bomber Command. To this day, no government will agree to strike a special campaign medal to honour the bravery of the men of that Command.

So please read on and I hope that by reading the story of my personal experiences with the early RAF bomber force you too will understand the strength of feeling amongst Bomber Command veterans.

144 Squadron, July 1940.

CHAPTER ONE
"The Day War Broke Out"

My generation will always remember these words, once uttered by that loveable old comedian Rob Wilton in describing all the amusing things which happened to him on that momentous day, but to many thousands of others they bring back far more serious memories.

Let me first take you back to the days before the war, when it was painfully obvious that whatever we did to appease Hitler, and in spite of Prime Minister Chamberlain's assurances of "peace in our time", war with Germany became increasingly inevitable.

Youngsters, many fresh out of school, flocked to the reserve organisations which had been set up by the various branches of the armed services, and my choice early in 1939 was the RAF Volunteer Reserve, to train as an Air Observer.

Pilot training was available, but one has to remember that in pre-war days, RAF pilots were the elite, being either regular RAF officers or members of the somewhat exclusive Auxiliary Air Force, which had squadrons linked with the larger cities or Universities. These officers were the blond, blue-eyed, supermen who put up superb flying displays at the pre-war Hendon air displays and to our simple minds there was just no way that we could ever enter their world. We were of course totally wrong, because when circumstances demanded, it was proved that intelligent young men from all walks of life could be trained and would, in most cases, become a very able pilots.

Opposite page: Hawker Hart flight trainer.

Mind you, even then, some pilots still assumed such an attitude of superiority that other aircrew members found the need to bring them down to earth. We would refer to them as "drivers, airframe" – that usually did the trick.

The Air Observer was a kind of super navigator in that, with the small crew complement, he was responsible for navigation, reconnaissance, photography, bombing and even an element of gunnery.

Trainees were given the rank of Leading Aircraftman (LAC) with promotion, eventually, to at least the rank of Sergeant, once fully operational.

Ground training was carried out at so-called 'Town Centres', in my case in London at a unit alongside Dolphin Square, close by the Tate Gallery, whilst such flying as was possible was carried out at Stapleford Abbots aerodrome to the north-east of London. We were paid one-shilling (5p) for each hour spent at lectures, plus half as much again when we flew. Never mind, we were now flying at the Government's expense, though little did we realise what a high price would eventually be paid by many of us.

Until 'the powers that be' got to grips with the need for, and value of, air crew, wireless operators and air gunners were, in many cases only ranked as Aircraftmen 2nd class and were not even awarded a brevet. In fact the air gunner had a brass winged bullet on his sleeve to denote his task, whilst the wireless operator had a cloth badge on his sleeve.

At least Air Observers wore a brevet, which was an oval badge with a half wing attached, irreverently and for obvious reasons christened 'the flying arsehole'! As the war progressed, all aircrew other than pilots were given a badge comprising a small wreath, with a half wing attached and enclosed within it, a letter or letters signifying their duty i.e., N, AG, etc.

My early navigation training took place in the Hawker Hart, a high speed, extremely manoeuvrable bi-plane, but there was little real training that one could undertake jammed into the rear of one of the two open cockpits with all the noise in creation going on, little or no communication with the pilot and a map which did it's best to disappear over the side. Map reading was just about the limit of what was possible, but it was a challenge and fun. I should mention that in the few weeks preceding the outbreak of hostilities, the unit was delighted to take delivery of the first of its 'mighty' Avro Ansons.

The Anson was a twin-engined cabin-style machine, already in use with Coastal Command, but of course, in our case, it did not have the operational gun turret. Never mind, for the short period we were able to fly in it, it was sheer pleasure to be able to sit in a cabin, to have the luxury of a chart table, and to welcome a wireless operator on board. It was still rather noisy, but at least a heating supply was available.

However, there is always a price to pay, and in this case it involved the undercarriage, for our newly acquired aeroplane had retractable wheels. Sadly, these were not hydraulically operated and had to be wound up and down by hand. I can't recall the precise number of turns of the control handle, but it was somewhere in the region of 150 backbreaking movements. Who else to carry out that task but the trainee Air Observer? That wasn't all, for on our return to land, the same unfortunate soul had to carry out the reverse drill. It was a great muscle-building exercise and even took the mind away from any feelings of airsickness, which were certainly prevalent in those early days.

Training progressed at a leisurely pace until, as September approached, one could see the storm clouds gathering, and on September 1st, it all happened.

First came a radio announcement that all reservists should report to their headquarters units, in uniform. There was panic at home as I donned the coarse blue/grey uniform and assembled my few bits of Service equipment into my kit bag. A tearful farewell followed and then I was on the train to London. Arriving at Victoria Station, I headed south towards the river, joining a steady stream of similarly clad young men, obviously with the same destination.

We poured into the assembly hall, where there was hardly room to move and the din and excitement resembled a cattle market. The only person I recognised was the chap who had dealt with my attestation many months before, who went under the appropriate name of Sparrowhawk.

Then appeared the form and voice of a type we would get to know so well, and love or hate, in the years to come – the long-serving disciplinary Senior NCO. He entered from a door at the front of the hall, and bellowed at the top of his voice in a less than cultured voice.

"Shut up the bloody lot of you! Where do you think you are – a bleedin' Sunday School outing? And what the blue blazes are you doing here anyway?" One brave soul spoke up on our behalf, pointing out, somewhat sarcastically, that we hadn't turned up in strength from choice, but were responding to a general call out on the radio.

The response was swift, but unexpected.

"I don't know what the bloody hell you are on about, so you can all sod off home until I'm told!" On reflection, with so many reservists present, it took a brave man to make such a decision, but in the face of that order we had no option but to depart, and so in small groups, all engaged in animated conversation, we headed back towards Victoria Station.

One bright spark in my own group suggested that we drop in to a nearby pub and partake of a little light refreshment before setting off for home. The end product was one of the reasons why I shall always remember that day. I should point out that in those days, lager louts, vandalism and even sex of the uninhibited kind, were unheard of (indeed, a quick cuddle and squeeze of the hand in the back row of the cinema, was often frowned upon). Clean living, athletic young men, who held the opposite sex in awe, were the types which mums sought out for their daughters.

With very little cash between us, we descended into a cellar bar and ordered up. From then on the locals took over – 'fighting men just off to war' was how they saw us, and the evening didn't cost us a penny thereafter, or at least, as far as I recall, for totally unused to such quantities of alcohol, I rapidly faded away. I recall even less of the journey home, but it is for sure that I will always remember the day that, for me, war broke out.

What happened when the NCO at the town Centre reported his decision will never be known to we lesser mortals, but two days later an official envelope arrived ordering me to report to No.1 ITW at Cambridge and to use the enclosed rail travel warrant. So this was it. The war was on, and for me it would begin at Cambridge. Poor fool! How little I knew of the mysterious ways of the Royal Air Force! Yet it would not be long before my eyes were well and truly opened.

CHAPTER TWO

So It Begins... Well, Sort Of!

Armed with my warrant, dressed in full uniform, and with a half-filled kitbag slung over my shoulder, I arrived at Kings Cross station to find a whole host of similarly clad individuals, all sporting the white band around their forage caps that denoted trainee aircrew.

We poured onto the northbound train, and for many of us it was our first experience of a rail journey of any distance. Conversation in my compartment centred on possible reasons why we were going to Cambridge. There was certainly an aerodrome nearby, but that housed an aircraft manufacturing company.

On arrival we poured out into the forecourt with no semblance of order at all. This was soon rectified when one of 'those' NCOs arrived, except this time he was a Flight Sergeant sporting World War I medal ribbons. His upright figure, topped by a face obviously carved out of granite, caused a hush to settle over the assembled throng, whilst he and a group of accompanying Corporals surveyed us.

"Bloody hell! What do they expect us to do with a scruffy bunch of bastards like this!" were his first words to his escort. One hero in our midst saw this as an opportunity to sound him out on our immediate future and in a very cultured voice said, "Excuse me Sir, what are the plans for our stay here, because we are expecting to start flying right away."

Oh how I grew to love those old boys!

Opposite page: Westland Wessex.

"Flying? You bloody pansy! There'll be no bloody flying 'ere! We h'ain't got no h'aeroplanes, so we are going to teach you to march until you become real h'airmen – then maybe we'll show you an effing h'aeroplane!"

The truth being thus discovered, we were sorted into groups or 'flights' as they were known, each flight being given the name of one of the Colleges wherein we were to be billeted. Then, in some sort of loose order, we were marched off to join the air force.

We were here to learn discipline, to understand Service orders and regulations and to be pumped full of every known inoculation and vaccination substance, before being let loose into the RAF proper.

Whatever else, I think the one thing which most of us agreed stood us in good stead in the years to come was discipline, and for me that virtue, or call it what you will, remains invaluable.

Once we had settled in to the somewhat large college dormitories, for want of a better word, I soon realised what a mixed bag of characters I had joined. They came from all over the country, and all walks of life, but we all had one thing in common, a desire to fly and to use whatever skills we were about to be taught to smash Hitler and his Nazi hordes.

I recall well our many forays into the city and its multitude of pubs, coupled with the adoration of the local lasses who were delighted at finding hundreds of healthy young airman thrown into their midst.

I listened to endless hair-raising stories related by my comrades concerning their escapades with the opposite sex, and to my innocent mind it seemed that I had missed a lot thus far in my young life.

One chap, worldly wise by anybody's standards, offered to "fix me up with a popsie". I can't remember my agent's name, but he took me to a local pub, and warmed me up with a few "jars". He then led me to a somewhat blousy blonde, who gabbled away endlessly, dropping aitches left right and centre, at the same time persistently tapping me with her ample bosom, until, presumably when she thought I was "ready" and suggested that we depart for another place. That place happened to be a darkened bus shelter, where, as soon as we had seated ourselves, she flung herself across my lap sighing and muttering goodness knows what. My truly innocent mind concluded that she was now in some sort of primitive mating position, but I hadn't the foggiest idea of how to proceed and in any case I was frightened out of my wits. I bravely informed her that I had drunk far too much alcohol, and wished to return to Downing College, The 'lady' was far from pleased, and with my tail, or whatever, between my legs, I practically ran back to the college.

Although I did learn a little more of how one was expected to conduct oneself in the years ahead, it was a pretty pitiful start and I didn't enjoy it a bit!

We marched, drilled, learned about the King's Rules and Regulations, took on board the dangers of VD (in fact one or two of the lads learned about it at first hand) and above all else we learned precisely how to deal with those hoary old NCOs, who had us believe that we were all "poofs, pansies and layabouts" – totally unsuitable for "their" Royal Air Force.

Inevitably the day came, when we were paraded and informed that posting notices were through. In my case I was destined to move to the Air Navigation School at Hamble in Hampshire. This was a pretty good spot at which to start, for that particular school had been operating for a number of years under some sort of Empire Air Training scheme.

I say start, but after a while I began to wonder what the pre-war training was for, since it appeared that we were about to go over the same ground again and indeed that was precisely what happened, although it was now to be in a more thorough and co-ordinated form.

Like all journeys by rail in wartime, particularly at night, the trip down to London was dark and dismal. Windows blacked out, no heating; little or no attempt to keep compartments clean and the all-pervading residual body odours, which seemed to have sunk into the upholstery.

It was a relief to leave that behind and, after a quick journey across the Capital, to join a fast Southern Railway train to Southampton Central.

A small group of us off-loaded ourselves in the early hours and searched for our transport to Hamble. Lesson 1: 'never take anything for granted' – there was no transport. A quick telephone call to the guardroom at the base produced the answer that we were not expected until later and had no option but to wait until the motor transport section came to life, unless of course we would care to walk. A typical example of the lack of organisation that prevailed in those early days. Kitbags slung over our shoulders, we set off, briefed by a porter to follow the road past Netley Hospital and on down to the aerodrome.

Tired and disgruntled, we finally caught sight of the aerodrome, but there to lift our spirits, were real live aeroplanes. However, as we were to find out in due course, many of them really belonged in aviation museums... but more of that later.

Reporting to the guardroom, since there were no signs of life elsewhere, we were despatched to a village hall a short distance away where we found the typical service metal beds, a pile of blankets on each, and even sheets and a pillow. Without guidance, we all did our best to make up the beds and in a short space of time quiet descended over the hall as tired and weary airmen drifted off into well-earned sleep.

Sleep may well have been well-earned, but it didn't last long, for after what seemed to be a few short minutes, a massive figure flung open the door and at a volume which would have deafened the RSM at Sandhurst, roared, "Come on you lazy layabouts! You're in the Air Force now! Time to get out on parade!"

His attempt at humour was ill timed to say the least but he was yet another of those who were to be obeyed, so grumbling and grousing, we unpacked kit bags, took his guidance on ablutions and wearily set about preparing ourselves for the short trip up to the aerodrome, where in fact he advised us the we had to go through the 'reporting in' procedure as soon as the Orderly room and staff opened up.

This procedure of 'reporting in' was something which we became quite accustomed to over the years, but it invariably gave rise to a host of irritating problems stemming from lost documents, incorrect dates or Service numbers, none of which would arise in this age of the computer... I think!

A while later, in very loose formation, we accompanied our new 'friend' along the road to the main gate. On the way, we could see across the fields to the aerodrome proper and there they were – Britain's war planes. What a collection! First there was the Avro Anson, last seen at Stapleford Abbots, with, standing alongside it, two of it's predecessors, the Avro 652, a similar type of machine but being totally enclosed, cabin style. Then there were several Airspeed Envoys, which preceded the Airspeed Oxford. The Oxford was a machine used extensively in twin-engined pilot training later on, but the crunch came when we saw Hamble's pride and joy, two Westland Wessex aircraft. These were tri-motor aeroplanes which did not look unlike the German Junkers transport, though smaller, probably closer in appearance to the American triple engined model, used on their transcontinental pre-war mail runs.

Whatever it looked like, it was a pain as far navigation training was concerned for, apart from the noise, the centre engine used to pour oil over the windscreen, making forward vision almost impossible. However, I'm getting a bit ahead of myself.

Having checked ourselves in, we were split into smaller groups of twelve, given Class numbers and marched off to various classrooms where we were met by our teams of tutors. In my case I immediately recognised a Mr Wells who had been an instructor at Town Centre, but the remainder of our teachers were service personnel wearing civilian clothing, plus one or two former Imperial Airways staff who would deal with certain aspects of flying.

The syllabus looked frightening, comprising navigation, meteorology, tactical flying, radio aids, instruments, aerial photography and reconnaissance plus a few other allied subjects.

Our first step was to assemble outside where the mandatory group photograph was taken. This photograph attests to the appallingly low survival rate of wartime aircrews. Only two of those present made it through to see final victory.

Before commencing lectures we were informed that the pilots who were to fly us around during our training were a mixed bag of serving NCOs, a couple of pilots from smaller pre-war civil airlines and one or two veterans from Imperial Airways.

The general idea was that we would receive navigation instruction in classroom and then before we had a chance to forget, we were required to leap into the air next day and consolidate that information.

One problem was that most of the early navigation techniques, other than basics, were linked to marine practices and procedures. So it was that we were taught how to intercept a naval vessel that was following a specific course, when we had no vessels on tap to practice with. The answer was to require us to get airborne at Hamble and, armed with the knowledge of the time that the Exeter to Bristol train left Taunton, to calculate a precise time and point at which we would intercept it, plus which we were given a massive hand held camera to produce photographic evidence of this interception.

Dare I say it, but even then the trains did not run on time, so any calculation would be of little use. Even though we were only beginners, we used our initiative and flew well up the line ahead of the train and then turned back down-line until we met it, to take the vital photograph – and this was supposed to be preparation for eventual flying with Bomber Command – I ask you!

It wasn't until later that we were introduced to the delights of flying in the Westland Wessex, in which, as I recall, I was frightened out of my wits before we even took off. Climbing into this museum piece was rather like joining a speciality ride at the local fairground, noise beyond belief as the three engines were started up, hanging on for dear life during the take off run, and then, since they were used for cross country map reading exercises, doing one's best to view the ground from a side window, forward vision being marred by the outpouring of oil from the centre engine which plastered the windscreen. Perhaps I exaggerate a little, but it was bad. When I look back and study photographs of that aeroplane, I find it difficult to see how we coped, but they were dire days and we all had to adapt.

We also began to undertake navigation exercises of a different type using the Avro 652, a much more comfortable aircraft although it had a heating system which matched that of a tropical hothouse. By itself this was not too bad, but when combined with a new found problem it spelled disaster. I refer to airsickness, which in noisy, somewhat unstable aeroplanes was common. The solution was to provide all trainees with a large dollop of solid glucose; somewhat like the doses of cod liver oil and malt which pre-war mums used to shovel into their offspring. The theory was that gravity would take the glucose down and hold it so that no food previously consumed could possibly find it's way up again. That was fine in theory, but even in modest temperatures, and with some turbulence, things began to bubble up.

There was a floor hatch in the 652 which, when raised, revealed a piece of equipment called a drift sight which, when properly used, gave the navigator an indication of just how much the aeroplane was drifting left or right of its intended track, so that corrective action could be taken.

Sad to say, the hatch was used for an entirely different purpose, since as soon as things began to move up the digestive system, the sufferer made a dive for the hatch, lifted it and poured glucose and whatever else, over the Hampshire countryside. Several of us managed to hold the feeling of sickness at bay, but as soon as any one trainee succumbed, it spun off and almost inevitably we all joined in a kneeling posture for purposes other than assessing drift. Things improved slowly as we became more accustomed to the heat and aircraft motion.

The exercises which we undertook were to practice dead reckoning navigation, known always as 'DR'. Armed with the Met Man's prognostications we were required to fly a number of compass headings, whilst by devious means we endeavoured to update the latest wind speed and direction information. Armed with this, we then had to calculate our assumed position and consequently provide a heading back to base. For understandable reasons, weather forecasts in those days were not very accurate, added to which our own attempts at updating usually proved to be well wide of the mark, hence, at the time we had estimated for our arrival over the destination, we were usually elsewhere. It was often said, with tongue in cheek, that we were 'temporarily unaware of our position' when in truth we were lost. The resultant panics and recoveries taught us a lot and certainly no one could ever be said to have been overconfident at Hamble.

Inevitably frustration began to set in, because although we were learning fast, we felt that we ought to be elsewhere, 'having a go' at the Nazis.

Propaganda was such that we were unaware that, in fact, not a lot was going on as regards operations at that time. The RAF was still participating in the 'phoney war' and flights over enemy territory were made solely to drop propaganda leaflets, whilst bombing was confined to coastal military targets or naval vessels, the official thinking being that if we didn't attack and damage their civilians, they wouldn't respond in a like-for-like campaign. What a laugh that was when you consider what followed soon after!

That apart, our morale was high and a tremendous sense of national pride prevailed. I recall an evening lecture and slide show given by a Squadron Leader Godsave, a veteran RAF Officer, covering prewar RAF operations on the North West Frontier and in Iraq, the last slide to be projected showing a group of airmen standing below the Union Jack and saluting. Godsave proudly announced that this was "the reason for it all", which drew tremendous applause and demonstrates the sense of national pride to which I have referred. Add to this the stirring speeches of Winston Churchill, not to mention his insults to Hitler, and one can understand why we were itching to get on with the job.

Of course, we also needed relaxation, and this was provided by the pubs in Hamble village, one of the most popular being The

Bugle, alongside the river. We made friends with the few local residents, likewise with the barmaids, although the latter were in greater demand in short supply. We rarely got beyond the village; there simply wasn't time.

Realising that only success would ensure an early posting, we all knuckled under, and results in ground school and in the air were extremely promising, so much so that the Chief Instructor hinted at a move in the near future. Sure enough, after one of the early morning parades, we were divided off into groups of six to eight and given the good news. The nominated units gave a clue to our futures, with some destined for Army Co-operation squadrons, others for Coastal Command and in the case of my little group, Bomber Command. We were destined for yet another training unit, this time to the Bombing and Gunnery School at Penrhos, in North Wales.

I always suspected that posting dates in the RAF were based on bad weather forecasts, for on almost every occasion on which I was moved, it seemed to rain, except one occasion when my group ventured north in what seemed to be solid drizzle, giving one hundred percent humidity.

The combined farewell party that was held at the Dolphin Hotel in Southampton followed what was to become the pattern for all future such events. Suffice it to say that it was a memorable evening – we all became delightfully 'sloshed' but with no vandalism, no breakages and no fights. My, how times have changed!

Our journey north, at night, was like so many others in those days: cold weather, windows blacked out, no heating in the compartment, body odours and the stench of stale tobacco, yet we managed to overcome these problems with youthful humour and stoicism. Our stop at Crewe was our only real comfort en route, when those lovely ladies of the various women's organisations moved along the train and bombarded us with mugs of steaming hot tea and cheese rolls. They did so much for morale and deserved all the praise which ultimately came their way.

Similarly, our journey from the rail terminus to the aerodrome was made in the wet and dark, and we were finally met by a very disgruntled Corporal at the Guard Room who conducted us to the wooden barrack block which would be our home, together with another twelve or so new arrivals, until we had perfected those skills which we were about to be taught. So started the next phase of our part in the long road to victory.

The Fairey Battle.

CHAPTER THREE

Practice Bombs
but Real Bullets

After our period of communal living at Hamble, sharing space with around 20 strangers in our new accommodation presented very few problems, partly because we had begun to adjust to Service life, but also because, although we were a mixed bag, we had a common aim. We were volunteers who lived and trained for the day when we would become fully operational and could get on with that which we knew had to be done.

The nearest town was Pwllheli, which I am told is now a popular holiday spot, but it was far from being so in 1940. The only attractions were the odd pub or two and the local fish and chip shop, none of these being sufficiently attractive to entice us out, other than on special occasions.

Evenings were spent in playing cards, mainly whist, for we had yet to learn the challenges of poker, and as training progressed there was a need for evening study, which was better conducted in groups.

Strangely enough, we learned quite a bit about life in general from our elder brothers in khaki, the Pioneer Corps, who had been posted in, presumably to guard the camp and carry out general 'dogsbody' duties.

They would call in and join us in the evening and regale us with stories of Army life, past and present, often reducing us to tears of laughter. They made it very clear, having seen our sleeping arrangements, which included sheets, just how fortunate we were, although when I reflect upon what awaited us in the years ahead, I wonder if, had they known, they would still have envied us.

Incidentally, in those days, we were provided with an iron bed-frame with very basic springing, upon which we had to place the mattress. Not a conventional mattress but three so called 'biscuits', each around two to three feet square which were butted together on the springs and eventually held in place by tucking blankets underneath each side and at the bottom, having first laid them over the top, of course. Much has been said of aircrew and their sheets but I reckon they were well earned.

In the early days, when discipline was all-important, there was a ritual to 'making up' after rising. Biscuits had to be stacked at the head of the bed, sheets and blankets neatly folded in standard shape and the whole wrapped in another blanket, making one neat package, and woe betide you if it wasn't so on inspection! I'm not too sure what this did for the war effort, but I guess it helped to keep new boys in line.

Ground school was most interesting, because now we were to learn about the armament side of our future roles. First we were taught the component parts of the Lewis machine-gun, almost a museum piece even then, and how to strip down and reassemble it, hopefully in the right order. Where is the ex-aircrew man who cannot remember such vital parts as the rear lever, keeper, retainer and spring? We then moved on to the Vickers gas-operated machine gun, slightly more modern but, as we soon discovered, just as likely to jam in flight, hence we learned to strip that down too. Mind you, I don't recall any trainee being required to do so in flight, for reasons I will explain later. It was also necessary to learn how to deal with firing at a target moving on the beam, and to allow a certain amount of deflection. Any thoughts of 'hosepiping' were ruled out since ammunition wasn't cheap.

There then followed a series of lectures on spraying techniques, using large canisters of an unknown substance. This procedure was codenamed Smoke Curtain Installation (SCI) although I have no idea why.

We were required to take note of prevailing weather conditions and then to determine height and heading to ensure covering a specific area. Since there was no requirement for crop spraying in those days, I leave the reader to deduce, if he or she can, what this was all about but thank goodness I can think of no occasion when there was a call for it's application.

We were then introduced to the so-called Course Setting Bomb Sight (CSBS), which consisted of a normal compass bowl with relevant fittings, a vertical fold down graduated bar, holding a sighting device and a forward protruding bar, also graduated, with another sighting point.

It is not possible to elaborate here, but you must visualise that the aimer, having set up essential values on the various scales, directed the pilot onto a target, and when this appeared in line with the vertical and horizontal sights, pressed a release button and uttered those oft quoted words "bombs gone".

It required more than one mistake in the air before I took on board the fact that a small sighting error on the bombsight meant a significant error on the ground.

Incidentally, it wasn't all work and no play, because at weekends we were given time off and a small group of us used to wind down by trekking westwards to the beautiful bay and coastal area around Llanbedrog.

Now to the aeroplanes in which we flew; this time they were all regular Service aircraft, albeit, in one case, somewhat dated.

Gunnery was carried out from the Hawker Demon (developed from the Hart in which I had flown pre-war), bombing from the Fairey Battle and an introduction to a form of gun turret in the Handley Page Harrow.

Because of the amusing problems and difficulties which occurred during this stage of our in-flight training, I will tell you a tale or two of what went on.

The Fairey Battle was still being used operationally, although the squadrons equipped with this aeroplane took a heavy mauling in France before the evacuation, and it would do a lot of good for youngsters of today's world to read how the first two VCs in the RAF were earned when Battles attacked the bridge at Maastricht, and pilot Garland and his navigator Gray, together with their wireless operator, died attempting to destroy the bridge in order to hold up the German advance. At first glance, the Battle had the appearance of a Hawker Hurricane that had been stretched, but although it had the same engine, the Rolls Royce Merlin, it was badly underpowered and was replaced as quickly as possible.

When flown on operations, the Battle carried a crew of three, the pilot, a navigator and a wireless operator/air gunner, but when used for training there was no requirement for the radio man since we rarely flew more than a short distance from Penrhos.

With ground school lectures tucked away, the great day came to put theory into practice. I met up with the staff pilot who was to take me on my first bombing 'mission' and having checked that the requisite number of practice bombs had been loaded, and that the bods at the bombing range a few miles to the west (appropriately named Hell's Mouth) were ready to sight and record my bomb bursts, I hoisted myself into the rear of this mighty machine and stood by for take off.

The practice bombs were a standard type, weighing eleven and a half pounds and contained a chemical which produced a white "puff" on impact, so that the aimer and the range officer could both plot the point of impact.

With little or no preliminaries, we roared across the airfield, took to the air and headed off to the range. I duly took myself down into the bowels of the machine, where the bombsight was mounted over a plastic floor hatch, which obviously had to be opened to provide clear vision during the run in to the target.

The pilot meanwhile headed directly for the target, which consisted of a large white painted triangle, mounted on stilts. Before attempting to bomb, the drill was to fly on three different headings, roughly one hundred and twenty degrees apart and to assess the drift on each. Using the bombsight, and a prescribed plotting process, it was then possible to establish the local wind speed and direction at our height and thereby provide accurate information to set on the sight.

Unfortunately, this required drawing lines on the compass bowl using a chinagraph pencil, rather like a crayon. The bomb sight being located just to the rear of the engine, as soon as the hatch was opened, a blast of extremely hot air poured in, and whilst this may have been of comfort on a very cold day, it also melted or softened the core of the pencil, making it was virtually impossible to draw the requisite lines. Abandon the exercise? Not a bit of it! The wise student had obtained a forecast wind value before take off and used that to good effect.

I was somewhat disheartened at first when my bombs dropped wide of the mark, but once I had learned that precision sighting was essential, my bombs began to drop closer to the target. It was explained to us later that we should bear in mind that the bomb which came close, yet missed, was not a disaster, for when the time came to drop the real thing, our bombs would be dropped as a 'stick', that is a number in quick succession, and today's near miss could be tomorrow's strike.

On our return, there were frequent differences of opinion with the range officer, since with several aeroplanes bombing in quick succession, results could become mixed and there were many scraps during which navigators claimed the best results as their own and the bad ones as the other chap's. It made little difference, as the staff were well up to those tricks and made their own assessments. In spite of all, I was delighted to find, at the conclusion of my training, that I had achieved an above average assessment, although, as I found out in due time, this was of little value – the run up to a heavily defended enemy target proved to be a trifle less stable, to say the least.

Gunnery training was almost farcical and I still chuckle when I think back to the manner in which it was conducted. On paper, we were to draw circular cans of .303 ammunition, load up our guns before take off, jump into the Hawker Demon biplane and head off to the gunnery range where the target towing aircraft would be waiting. He would be towing an open drogue, rather like the windsock seen at aerodromes. We, for our part, would fly on a parallel course to the towing aircraft, and at an agreed distance off, and at a given signal, open fire, hoping optimistically to hit the drogue. That was the plan, but in reality... 'Oh my gawd!'

The Demon had two cockpits, one for the pilot and a rear one for another crew member. The rear position was contained in a primitive form of power-operated turret, which turned in a horizontal plane, and when the gun was lowered in angle, a protective screen, rather like an armadillo's shell was raised behind the crew man, lowering behind him again as the gun was elevated. Another innovation was to add a form of paint, different colours, to each can of ammunition so that, in theory, several gunners could fire on one drogue, and the number of 'hits' could be credited to each man on the basis of colour. It simply didn't work in practice, maybe because of the quality of the paint or simply because it wasn't workable in the first place. There were endless arguments after the exercises, but one gained the impression that no one really cared as long as there were enough bullet holes to share out.

My own initiation commenced when a fresh-faced young sergeant pilot invited me to clamber aboard and, as it happened, suffer the shock of a lifetime.

As he clambered aboard I was reminded of the old films of World War I air battles over the trenches, for here was a man clad in flying suit, leather helmet and gauntlets, goggles ready to pull down, and shiny leather flying boots to round it all off. He hauled himself over the side and motioned to me to clamber into my position, which I did, fitting the ammunition pan over the gun before settling in. There was no intercom such as existed later during the war, merely a system called, I believe, a 'Gosport tube' which was very similar to the systems found on older naval vessels and even in Victorian kitchens. To be truthful, the only in flight communication, which could not be affected by the overall noise was a system of hand signals. Thumbs up meant the obvious, and a clenched fist shown to the pilot signified a malfunction of the gun.

Anyway, signifying to the gent up front that I was as ready as I was ever likely to be, he started up the engine which responded with a mighty roar and a burst of blue smoke. The ground crew man pulled away the wheel chocks and the game was on. Unlike the sedate procedures at Stapleford Abbots, this pilot headed straight into wind opened the throttle and away we shot. Once airborne, he put this lively little machine into a steep climb and headed for the sun, although this procedure was really unnecessary, as the range was only a short distance away. As I discovered later, this behaviour was merely evidence of the frustration which affected many of the staff pilots who wanted nothing more than to get away and join an operational unit in Fighter Command, as I had already deduced, from their style of flying.

With the wind screeching through the wing struts, plus the apparent instability of the machine, I clutched the sides of the cockpit and held on. The bay at Hell's Mouth appeared below, and at the same time I discovered that the strange noise I could hear in the background was the pilot shouting down the voice tube and pointing off to one side.

I couldn't hear a word hence I did the only thing, which seemed appropriate at the time, I put my thumb up. Off to starboard, I now saw the towing aeroplane, and well aft of him was the target drogue. My pilot commenced a wide turn and then settled on a parallel heading to the other machine, gaining on him very slowly.

My duty was clear, first I pointed the gun seawards and let off a few rounds, then gave a thumbs up to the pilot, who had turned to see what the noise was all about.

Now the proud moment, as I slowly rotated the primitive turret and directed the gun towards the target, remembering to allow for 'deflection' since it was moving relative to us. Target in the fore and back sights, finger on the trigger, and just as I was about to fire, the gun mounting began to drift slowly back towards the rear of the aircraft. Then I remembered, we had been told that the system, hydraulic I think it was, could not always sustain the required pressure to hold it in place, hence the drift back. I made a sign to the 'driver' who obviously didn't understand, but commenced another turn to make a fresh run up. This time, as the drogue hove into view, I was prepared and rotated the unit until the gun was now pointing well ahead. As I commenced firing, I thought 'Gotcha you brute! Drift back now and I'll pepper the target.' Of course, this time it didn't drift, and my shots went whistling ahead of the target towards the Irish Sea.

Head turned towards me, the pilot was again shouting instructions, and although I could not understand him, it was not difficult to deduce that whatever he was saying was not complimentary. Pointing towards the drogue, he slipped our aeroplane towards it until we were in a position where I could almost autograph the canvas. I then caught the word "Fire!"

I couldn't disobey, and poured a long burst into the poor target until I had 'emptied the can'. Feeling a little better about things, I thought, "Now, back we go," but not a bit of it! This was the moment 'Flash Gordon' had been waiting for, and with a yell (which I could hear clearly) he opened the throttle and threw the aeroplane into a tight turn. For the next ten minutes or so we engaged in a series of aerobatics which would have earned him praise at any air show. I confess that I closed my eyes more than once, and the G forces, even in that small aircraft, thrust me time and time again, down into the seat.

Eventually, the fuel supply dictated that he return to Penrhos, but by that time I was past caring. Walking back to the office after landing I was simply grateful to be alive. I ventured to suggest that this really wasn't why I had been sent to B&G school, to which his reply was that he hadn't wanted to come here to fly bloody trainees either. I reckon that these flights – and there were others of a similar nature – could at least go down as 'air experience'. But what an experience!

Like all things, one soon adapted, knowing that if an air exercise had to be aborted, aerobatics would almost inevitably follow, and some even grew to enjoy these 'interludes'. Being young and lusty, rumour has it that the RAF concealed bromide in our diet to curb our desires, but the one thing which was unnecessary was a laxative as flights such as that referred to above kept our bowels in good order!

In all the excitement of bombing and gunnery, our thoughts had drifted away from the reason for it all, but all too quickly for some, the chief ground instructor announced that posting notices were on the way.

Sure enough, they were duly announced and most of us, in small groups, were scheduled for OTUs (Operational Training Units) where we would use all that we had been taught and apply it whilst operating on a specific type of aeroplane.

In my case, I was to be posted to No.17 OTU at Upwood in Huntingdonshire, where I would apply my skills, such as they were, in the Mark 1 Bristol Blenheim, a short-nosed version of this type. The Blenheim was a medium range twin-engined bomber, at that time engaged on daylight operations.

Quite a few of the staff at Upwood had only recently converted to the Blenheim, having previously served on Fairey Battle squadrons in France, where they had suffered heavy losses, so that they were already 'blooded', with more than a story or two to tell, but doubtless mighty relieved to be flying a more powerful and reliable machine.

Once again, kit bags packed and railway warrants issued, we were on our way, and furthermore – joy of joys – on arrival we were to be promoted to Acting Sergeant/Acting Observer and don the much envied flying brevet at long last.

Bristol Blenheim Mark I (above) and Mark IV (below).

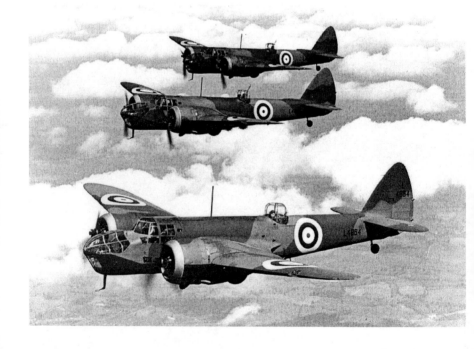

CHAPTER FOUR

Almost the Real Thing

Arrival at Upwood followed the usual procedures, except that now we were accommodated in pre-war barrack blocks and each had the luxury of a room to himself. Firstly, we were issued with three stripes to signify our promotion to Sergeant, if only 'acting' for the present, then at long last we received the Air Observer's brevet. I for one, assumed a new sense of pride. How typically British though, that instead of a formal Wings Parade, during which a Senior Officer made the presentation, as per the US Army Air Corps system, we simply drew our badge from the stores and each did his best to sew it on, apart from those who were fortunate enough to have WAAF lady friends, who proudly did the job for them.

True, there was still an element of training to be completed, but now we were in an atmosphere where everyone seemed to move with a sense of purpose. The aeroplanes were fully equipped and armed, and we were in Bomber Command territory where we soon witnessed overflying aircraft on their way to war.

As an NCO, my room was at the end of a barrack room, and I was informed that I would be held responsible for basic discipline in those quarters.

I had never been briefed on such duties, and knowing how green I was, the airmen tended to take liberties, but after threatening to put offenders "on a charge", not that I really intended to do so, this did help and things settled down to an acceptance of each other's duties and responsibilities.

As a new boy, I came in for tasks that had nothing whatsoever to do with flying training. Each aerodrome had an identification light beacon, which, using a bright red neon light, flashed letters in Morse code, such as, for example, UP for Upwood. These beacons, code named Pundits, could not be sited at the aerodrome lest the Luftwaffe attack the site, yet they had to be somewhere close by, otherwise their function would have been pointless. Newly arrived aircrew were provided with a driver, an electrician and sets of blankets. Boarding a lorry, we towed the beacon to one of a number of pre-selected sites, where the beacon would be switched on at sunset to stay on, flashing all night, to assist those up above who had little else to aid them in determining their position.

It was a thankless job, often undertaken in cold, damp conditions and certainly with little sleep, but many months later, I was to learn at first hand the great value of these visual aids.

One bonus, much appreciated, was that we were now members of the Sergeants Mess, with ready access to a comfortable lounge, the billiard room and the bar. Although members of my group were not the first newly appointed 'upstarts' to join the Mess, many of the 'old sweats', who had spent years struggling to reach Senior NCO status, bitterly resented our rapid promotion and made their feelings known. This led to an element of tension, but as the operational demands on aircrew began to grow, and losses took place, an air of appreciation and understanding started to develop. Eventually, as the war progressed, the bonds between air and ground crew became very strong indeed, as each learned how one needed to lean heavily on the other from time to time.

After a short spell of ground school I was ready to start flying in the Mk 1 Blenheim, a fast machine but not particularly comfortable, since this was the short-nosed version in which the navigator sat alongside the pilot and endeavoured to carry out his duties using a 'Bigsworth board' (something like a draughtsman's board) upon which the map was placed. The Wireless Operator/ Air Gunner sat in the rear below a small turret, although on training flights there was no call for its use, efforts being concentrated on dealing with radio communications.

The limited navigation facilities did not matter because pretty well all of our exercises were simulated low-level attacks, where the essential skill was to be able to map read with accuracy and basic navigation theory was cast aside.

All flying was undertaken in daylight. We were usually sent off to the west and then expected to drop down below 1,000 feet and return, flying at low level, to 'attack' a designated target, maybe a town or aerodrome, and bring back photographic proof of success. For this purpose we were given a new type of low-level bombsight and a very expensive Leica camera.

Low level map reading, at speed, was particularly difficult, as unless one kept one's gaze fixed to the ground at all times, the slightest loss of concentration, and unidentifiable ground features started to rush by, and panic would set in. Two courses of action were then available to the poor lost soul. Having first let it be known that "we are lost", the options were to either climb up to a higher altitude and hope that the greater field of vision would enable one to pick up a landmark, and then return to a lower level and continue, or with great humility, turn to the radio man for help.

The help which he could provide consisted of two types of radio bearing, one known as a QDR, which was the magnetic bearing from the ground radio station which he had contacted, the other known as a QDM, was the magnetic course to steer to that same station. Both were obviously most useful, but there was a price to be paid, for in the Mess that evening there would be very few present who did not know that 'Sergeant X had got himself lost, but had been saved by Sergeant Y'. All good fun, but difficult to live with for a while!

Mind you, the radio men slipped up too, often as a result of endeavouring to provide assistance. It was necessary to use medium frequency radio for this purpose and in order to transmit a signal from the aeroplane which was powerful enough to be accurately detected and measured, the radio man had to wind out an aerial which really amounted to a long length of weighted wire, which trailed way behind the machine.

This process invariably worked, but problems arose when the wireless operator, doubtless flushed with success, at having "saved the navigator's bacon", forgot to wind the aerial back in again. This usually passed unnoticed until on final approach to landing a tremendous bang announced that the trailing aerial had snagged a tree or other obstruction, and parted company from the aeroplane. In such circumstances, honours were even, and the subject never came up for discussion in the Mess.

I truly enjoyed this phase of my training, although I had at the back of my mind the fact that daylight operations in recent months had led to quite a few casualties. So, my chums and I rapidly became proficient in the task set for us, although little did we know that, due to changing circumstances, we would never have occasion to put our knowledge and ability to use.

Towards the end of the training course we were required to carry out long distance night flights, again flying to the west, but this time returning at medium levels to simulate attacks on some of the cities in the Midlands. Obviously, there was no way that we could drop any types of bombs, so this had to be done in daylight at the nearest range which was at Wainfleet Sands on the north side of The Wash. Here, triangular targets were set on stilts in the sand or mud and we were required to bomb them, in most cases at low level. Many of our young pilots gave us problems by taking the term 'low-level' too literally, giving rise to tounge-in-cheek comments from the range officer that the idea was to fly over the targets and drop bombs on them, not to fly under them and hurl the bombs upwards!

Out of the blue, whilst still looking forward to more exciting low-level sorties, I was summoned to the Flight Commander's office and told that I had been selected for an immediate posting to No 101 Squadron, based at West Rainham, in Norfolk, to fly in the more up-to-date Mk.4 long-nosed version of the Blenheim.

This was basically the same aircraft, but the nose had been extended to provide an ideal position for the navigator, with a chart table on the port (left) side, a very comfortable seat, and pretty well all-round vision. I was, at long last, to be joining an operational unit, but as yet I had no idea of what its precise function was, although I was to learn that all too quickly, before departing from it in like manner very soon after.

It rarely paid to enquire, for example, why a lone soul like myself should suddenly be rushed off elsewhere, since in most cases "I have no idea" would be the answer. What I did learn, on arrival, was that I had been posted in to replace a crew member no longer available for reasons that were never explained to me. However, since the crew had been rostered for duty next day, I was truly 'thrown in at the deep end'. I cannot remember much about my fellow crew members, but I do remember the flight – a patrol over the North Sea end of The Wash, ostensibly to look for enemy shipping of any sort and to report back by radio – and I recall only too well the complete idiot I made of myself in my attempt to impress.

Heading out over a cold grey sea, with nothing in sight, I saw on the horizon, a vessel. As we closed on it, it was clearly one of the proverbial 'dirty British coasters' and so, since he seemed to be heading off to the south, I took it upon myself to pull out the Aldis signal lamp, and, directing it towards the vessel's bridge, spelled out "Good luck". Like a shot, he signalled back, and I informed the pilot that he was probably a foreign vessel, as he had signalled back the name "*Andtocou*". The words of derision from behind, coupled with a few with which I had already become familiar, casting doubts on my sanity and parentage, led me to believe that I had erred. Indeed I had, and the pilot pointed out that the reply from the ship was friendly, and simply said "And to you". There has to be a moral to this, but I'm not too sure what it was, except that I was at the wrong end of it!

Another lesson I learned at about the same time was to be ever-cautious of His Majesty's Royal Navy. Approaching the Humber estuary on one occasion, we observed a convoy assembling with a naval escort.

Ever mindful that they, not unreasonably, tended to be trigger happy, I sought permission to fire off the 'colours of the day'. To explain, all aircraft carried a Verey pistol with a variety of cartridges, each showing different colours on bursting. Every unit was given a specific cartridge for the day, say, for example, red and white on bursting. The theory was that 'our side' knew the appropriate colours, so when they were fired, they would automatically identify us as friendly. Duly, on this occasion, I fired off the correct colours as we approached. And what did the beloved matelots do in response? Shoot at us, of course!

There would be many times, returning back to Lincolnshire, that we would see convoys assembling in that same area, but from that day on we always kept at a safe distance, and left the 'colours of the day' safely stowed away.

My new posting lasted for only a very short period of time, because there very soon came an urgent call to increase crew numbers in No 5 Group of Bomber Command to replace heavy losses of aircraft that had resulted after misguidedly attempting daylight raids. There was a need for a major rethink, the end product of which was a switch to night raids. The aeroplane in question was the Handley Page Hampden, much beloved by most of those who flew her, and it was obvious that the change of tactics, requiring more aircraft, logically required more crews also. In the following chapter I will describe this fine aircraft in detail, but at that time it was a mystery to me – all I knew was that I had once again to pack my gear and this time make my way north-west to join No.106 Squadron at Finningley, close by Doncaster.

CHAPTER FIVE

The Real Thing

Arrival procedures followed standard practice, and I was quickly allotted a room at the end of a barrack block, told to unpack my gear and then drop into the Sergeants Mess for a meal, and in all probability, a drink with the 'lads'. The atmosphere in the Mess was one of friendship and enthusiasm, since the squadron was building up rapidly. Apart from comparative new boys like myself, there were quite a few 'blooded' veterans around to give moral support. The war hadn't been in progress long enough to produce hardened veterans, but some of our new colleagues had seen service in France and had taken part in coastal raids after the evacuation, so they knew what it was all about.

As far as the Hampden was concerned, we were all new boys and had to start from scratch. We were told that 106 Squadron was scheduled to become fully operational in a few weeks' time and all our training would be directed to that end, whatever category of aircrew we were.

The aeroplane had a very distinctive shape with all four crew positioned in a narrow box-like section at the front. Where this ended, the fuselage became a single long, thin boom, stretching out behind to finally join the tail unit which comprised what appeared to be two minute rudders. One look at it's shape in photographs explains why it was known as 'the flying suitcase' or even 'the tadpole'.

The pilot sat up in a reasonably spacious cockpit with a commanding view all round; in flight it was almost like sitting in a fighter aircraft. The Air Observer sat up front in a 'glasshouse' –

a fragile metal frame supporting masses of perspex. This gave certain advantages, but these were outweighed by disadvantages when over a target at night... But more of that later. In this position he had a hinged table, the bomb sight and related switches, a few basic instruments and finally a wrap around curtain which, in theory, prevented light from shining out at night, although the position also had red light bulbs in places which cut down on visible light whilst still enabling the navigator to work and – just as importantly – did not mar his night vision capabilities.

The Wireless Operator/Air Gunner sat in the rear top section of the aeroplane, where he had his radio equipment and two rear facing machine guns. These were pivoted to swing from side to side, with a metal guide bar in the centre which elevated the guns when pointing astern, thus preventing him from accidentally shooting the tail off. He also had a pull down perspex canopy, which could be lowered over his 'cockpit' when the guns or a lookout were not required. Down below him, in extremely cramped quarters sat the Air Gunner. His position was in a curved quadrant, shaped to round off the bottom rear end of the main section of the aeroplane, and from this mini glasshouse protruded another two pivoted guns. It was cold, cramped and claustrophobic, although the gunner could move back into the main fuselage, where he would then be behind the wireless man. The trouble was that the toilet, a portable Elsan, was sited there too, and although it got little use, since most of us had far too much on our minds once airborne, it still gave off a long remembered sweet and sickly aroma, which, when mixed with other aircraft smells such as fuel, oil and dope (Amyl Acetate) didn't do an awful lot to stave off feelings of air sickness!

In spite of the space problems, the Hampden was a good aeroplane in which to fly: it had reliable Bristol Pegasus engines, and excellent manoeuvrability and was fitted with Handley Page Wing slats, giving a low, safe landing speed.

We all had much to learn, and depending on the type of exercise we either carried a full crew of four or just a pilot and navigator, although most of us preferred to have a radio man on board in case we lost ourselves.

It was during these early stages of operational training that a number of serious accidents occurred. Oddly enough, they seemed to stem from the same problem. In order to raise or lower wheels and wing flaps the pilot had a single lever which he could move through an 'H' gate rather like the gear lever of a car. The drill was to bring hydraulic power on and then, immediately after take off, move the selector in to the wheels up position. Sadly, many pilots inadvertently moved it into the 'flaps up' position by selecting the wrong slot in the 'H' gate. This was disastrous, for the pilot now had no flaps to aid take off, the wheels were hanging down, the aeroplane was decidedly 'unclean' and headed pretty well uncontrollably straight for the ground – with the inevitable consequences. For many of us this was our first experience of losing friends and, in the circumstances, it was a dreadful waste of young lives.

I have often been asked how I can recall such events – and others which followed – in such detail. There is a twofold answer. Firstly, I still retain a comprehensive flying log book, together with target maps. For many of the raids, a quick glance at the record is usually all that is necessary to bring it vividly to mind. Secondly, like most of my colleagues, I had led a pretty sheltered life before joining the RAF and was very impressionable, so the traumatic events I experienced on raid after raid left their mark for all time.

Once we had accustomed ourselves to the aeroplane and it's equipment, the time came to commence the serious business of working up to operational status. There were numerous day and night cross-country flights, often to the northwest, out of harm's way, during which bombs of one sort or another were dropped, not live, of course. Several flights were made to Catfoss, just north of the Humber, where the gunners could use the air firing range to work off their frustrations, or whatever.

Our bombing range, if I remember correctly, was at a spot named Misson, not too far from Finningley, and there we were permitted the luxury of dropping 'sticks' of practice bombs plus, if we were very fortunate, one or two inert 250lb bombs. I do recall that on some of the local night flights, on which the crew consisted solely of the pilot and myself, the intense cold on board was hard to bear, even when wearing flying gear. There was a somewhat primitive heating system whereby hot air was passed down a corrugated flexible rubber tube. All one could do was to stuff the open end of this tube into any convenient opening in one's suit and then relax in comparative luxury.

The issue flying suits were a one-piece affair with pockets and zip-fasteners or press-studs everywhere. By the time this had been donned and various items such as equipment bags, parachute harness and chute were added, it was not easy to clamber down into the navigator's position in the forward section of the aeroplane without snagging one's clothing on the whole variety of bits and pieces which jutted out from the fuselage interior. We were given three pairs of gloves, known as 'gloves inner silk', 'gloves woollen' and 'gauntlets outer'. A fine collection, issued with the best of intentions, but how we were meant to handle navigation instruments whilst wearing that little lot was never made clear; even gunners found it hard enough. Once training had been completed, I was moved to 'B' Flight under the control of one Squadron Leader Parker, who informed me, quite casually, that the squadron was about to undertake it's first operational sortie, which he would be leading, and (lucky me) I was to form part of his crew. Now it was getting serious!

The raid would be undertaken by three aircraft, each carrying sea mines, and for my part, as a new boy, I would be relegated to the 'tin', as the bottom rear-gunner's position was known.

This was common practice in the early days when small bomber aeroplanes were used, because there was no means by which supernumeraries could be carried in order to gain experience. The same problem arose with pilots so that, in general, pilots operated for a trip or two as navigators, whilst the navigators, as already indicated, operated as under-gunners.

The advantage, so it was believed, was that once a crew member had been 'blooded', he knew what lay ahead and was better prepared to concentrate on his allotted task.

In the early stages of the war, the Hampden was the only aeroplane capable of carrying sea mines, which had to be dropped at low level and low speed – not a very pleasant experience at some of the German hot spots such as Keil harbour and approaches.

At long last the day came when we were called to an early afternoon briefing, prior to which the whole camp was alive with rumour. With only three aeroplanes taking part, the briefing was a low-key affair, and in due time the target was formally announced. We were to make our way independently to the mouth of the Gironde which runs down to Bordeaux, where we would deposit our gift and, hopefully, return. In those days, minelaying sorties were listed as 'nursery slopes', the mine was known as a 'vegetable' and the actual drop was coded as 'gardening'.

I never could understand the need for this form of coding, because the Germans were well aware of what we were up to, and if we turned up at a few hundred feet in a bay or estuary, they knew that we weren't there for the fishing. I suppose it gave someone in an office somewhere a feeling of satisfaction, and it did at least categorise the flights, although as I remember, they followed the same routine for bombing raids, at least at that time.

So the die was cast, and here I was about to take the war to the Hun. The aircraft had been flight tested earlier in the day, but, as a group, we wandered out to see the huge mine being hoisted into position. Since this was not to be an excessively long flight, and because everyone involved was running high on adrenaline, there was no question of retiring for a spell of rest, indeed the departure was to be in daylight, flying in loose formation until crossing the south coast at Chessil Bank where, with dusk coming on, we would break off and make our way independently to the target.

It was now mid-September 1940 and the thought did occur to me that here I was, almost a year after war had been declared, just about to take off on my very first operation – and even then it was not to be a bombing raid!

In late afternoon our small group of 12 (three 4-man crews) was given our final briefing, the main points of which were the latest weather information, the probable main sites of search-lights, anti-aircraft guns and night fighter airfields.

There was none of the drama associated with preparation as happened later on in the Command, and piling into the crew truck, we were driven out to three waiting aeroplanes, each of which had a small ground crew group standing nearby. Start-up and taxiing out to the take-off point were pretty much as if departing on a training flight, except that we could see several groups of well-wishers standing around the hangars to see us safely on our way. Being the Flight Commander's aeroplane, we were first off, and the one thing which became very apparent to me, sitting in the back and looking at the tail unit, was how it flexed in a very worrying fashion as the engine revolutions were increased for take-off.

The take-off run, with a heavy load, seemed to go on for ever, but eventually, after what seemed to be a desperate pull on the control column, the aeroplane left the ground and entered it's true environment. Engine revolutions were reduced to climbing power as the dear old Hampden climbed gently away. Looking back, I saw one of the other machines taking off and shortly afterwards both aircraft closed up on us.

We flew south, passing well to the west of London, and our pilot broke radio silence to advise the others that, with the coast ahead, they were now free to break the loose formation and make their own way. By now it was dusk, and our colleagues were slowly lost from sight as they took up their chosen headings for the target area.

This was one aspect of departures in those days which was difficult to understand since, quite frequently, crews were given specific points at which to leave the coast outbound, yet as they departed from that point, most seemed to head off in slightly different directions. This resulted from navigators carrying out individual calculations prior to departure, with variations in the end product. However, position checks on the flight enabled corrections to be made, and all seemed to reach their target satisfactorily.

I could see very little, sitting in the cold and dark at the rear, but after a while, conversation between pilot and navigator indicated that searchlights and tracer flie ahead gave a clue as to where they would cross the coast of occupied France. With visions of shot and shell, I was quite surprised as we did cross the coast, outlined in the dark by a white line of waves breaking on the shore, to see no more than a few searchlights wandering across the sky to the east, and one or two streams of tracer moving skywards

The reason for the comparative quiet was that we had been routed well to the west to avoid trouble on our first raid. Doubtless because I was with a very experienced pilot, nothing untoward occurred until I heard him advise us all to stand by, as he was about to commence a descent down to the appropriate height for the drop. As we drew closer to the sea, dark though it was, I could see white capped waves below, which signified that we were now at low level.

I found it hard to follow the conversation up front, but I gathered that the coast at the mouth of the Gironde had been identified and we were about to commence our run in. There was an increase in noise as the bomb doors were opened, and the next thing I heard were the words "OK, the bastards away!" I looked down quickly, but could see nothing. There was a sudden increase in engine-noise and G-force as the aeroplane was hauled round and put into a rapid climb.

It was then that I had my first close up of enemy opposition, for just behind us, what seemed to be a bank of searchlights suddenly lit up the sky, sweeping at very low level, though nowhere near horizontal, while at the same time a veritable firework display broke out as multi-coloured tracer shells formed snaking patterns in the sky. I was intrigued at how slowly the tracer appeared to move, until it came closer, when it rapidly accelerated, hopefully to pass harmlessly by. There was no heavy calibre gunfire directed at us and it was suspected that we had in fact been set upon by 'flak ships', which were sited in many estuaries. As we headed west, the tracer changed direction, presumably as our colleagues went about their business too.

For me, the whole flight was an anti-climax, since very little of what I had anticipated actually took place. Later on, after attacking major targets, I realised just how fortunate we had been with this first trip, particularly as it would count towards the total number of ops we were required to complete before we could be 'rested'... assuming that we survived, of course.

The flight back was uneventful, apart from the sight of London under attack as we flew by, well to the west.

In spite of the late hour, there were many waiting to greet us, and at the subsequent debriefing, all three crews provided sufficient detail for it to be agreed that each had completed their task satisfactorily.

For a few days, until the squadron was called upon to gear-up and participate to the full, our crews were regarded with awe.

I was never able to take part in that build up, because, yet again, I found myself on the move, thankfully to another more active Hampden squadron. I didn't realise it at the time, but there was a general move to transfer a large number of crew members to squadrons based around Lincoln. Lincolnshire was the home of Bomber Command's No 5 Group at that time, the main units being sited at Waddington, Scampton and Hemswell. Our 'Leader' at Group Headquarters was none other than Sir Arthur 'Butch' Harris, who at that time was an Air Vice Marshal, if I remember correctly. He had not yet built up the reputation which made him such a popular leader in the Command when things subsequently hotted up.

So here it was at last, a move to a fully operational squadron, which had already been heavily engaged in raids and had suffered losses, some very heavy, on recent sorties. There were two squadrons based at Hemswell, Nos 61 and 144 and I was posted to the latter.

It was not a long journey from Doncaster and when my small group arrived at Lincoln we found the usual drab coloured truck waiting to transport us, although we had first to await the arrival of those who had travelled from further afield. When names had been checked, the driver asked, in ominous fashion, if we were 'the replacements'. That didn't do a lot for our morale, as you may well guess.

Approaching the aerodrome in late afternoon, one gained an impression of 'business' at last, for dispersed around the perimeter were many aircraft, heavily camouflaged in green/brown on top, but matt black underneath to shield them from searchlight activity. Here and there, small tractors could be seen towing out lines of heavily-laden bomb trolleys, signifying that the squadrons were 'on' that night. For us, at least for the NCOs, it was a rapid move to barrack-block single rooms, followed by a meal in the mess. It was there that we obtained our first taste of active squadron life, for very few of the aircrew sitting around in the lounge were dressed in formal uniform, most wearing heavy-knit white sweaters, indicating that they were part of the team for the forthcoming raid that night. As always, we new boys or 'sprogs' – as we were known – were treated with an element of tolerance bordering on contempt, for we had yet to join their exclusive club, although that would come soon enough. So this was where it was all to start in earnest.

CHAPTER SIX

Off to 'Meet the Hun' at Last

Hemswell was one of the pre-war permanent stations which had most of the essential buildings formed around that vital part of any unit, the parade ground. Station Headquarters housed the administrative sections, and close by were the Officers and NCOs messes, both of which were fitted with comfortable anterooms containing billiard tables, a bar and dining room. The Sergeants mess was a mixed bag of well-disciplined long-serving group of Senior NCOs and a larger group of young upstarts whose rank came with their chosen appointment. Initially, there was an element of friction between these groups, but in due course, as the 'old sweats' saw the price which some of the youngsters paid, they mellowed in their attitude and a new feeling of tolerance and friendship developed – our war was with the Germans, not with each other.

Another nearby unit was the Station Sick Quarters, so called – although they had far more than sickness to deal with after some of the raids.

On reporting to 'the Flights' the day after my arrival, I was somewhat taken aback to learn that, even at this early stage, we were regarded as 'replacements' for those who had 'bought it' – airman's parlance for those who had not returned from operations for one reason or another.

I learned very early on that there was no time for grieving and that an outwardly callous approach was adopted following the

Opposite page: Bombing up a Hampden.

loss of a comrade, in order not to damage the morale of others, although few would deny that we all felt the hurt inside. Besides, any open form of grief would lead to despondency and fear, adversely affecting one's ability to give of one's best, the result being that your crew would then suffer with you if you failed to do your duty. So losses were acknowledged with a few words such as, "poor old Spud got the chop last night," or "Saw old Fred's plane coned by searchlights. Poor bastard was on fire when we looked back," or perhaps "Jock ran out of fuel on the way back. Poor sod came down in the drink." And so it went on. Plenty of bravado, but used to hide much deeper, unspoken feelings.

I was told that as a new boy, I would once again be relegated to 'the tin' and would be filling a slot in Sergeant King's crew, whoever he was.

Being already familiar with the Hampden, there was to be no introduction, so as soon as King was next listed for operations, then I would be too. He was, as it turned out, himself a comparative new boy, having only just completed his introductory flights as a navigator, so we were both pretty 'green'.

The next day, before lunch, the Tannoy (PA) system broadcast an announcement that all crews of 144 Squadron were to report for briefing at a given time, but that NFTs were to be carried out before then. The NFT (Night Flying Test) involved each full crew taking their aeroplane into the air and once in clear air space, everyone checked each item of equipment for serviceability. One had to be absolutely sure, as lives could depend on it later on. Once back on the ground, the team of engine fitters, riggers and armourers set about rectifying any reported problems.

Meanwhile, the first clue as to the nature of the forthcoming night's work would become apparent as the bomb trolleys trundled their way out to the aircraft dispersal points around the aerodrome. The normal load for a Hampden was four 500lb bombs in the bomb bay and two 250lb bombs, one below each wing, suspended from a bomb rack.

A fuse link attached to each bomb was also attached to the bomb rack, and just prior to dropping the bombs, the navigator had to operate a 'fuse selector switch'. This energised a solenoid on the rack so that as the bomb fell away, the link was held to the rack and hence pulled away from the bomb, thereby arming it.

There were other occasions, when different types of bombs were carried, as for example when attacking a naval vessel. In these circumstances an armour-piercing bomb would be loaded.

In a later chapter, I will detail the normal raid procedure from start to finish, but as this was not a normal raid for me, I will condense this story.

Briefing caused quite a stir when it was revealed that our the targets were to be the Krupps Armament factories at Essen, at the centre of a 'hot spot' – the vast industrial complex of the Rhur Valley. Even in those early days of the war, the Rhur was one of the most heavily defended targets in Germany and was known by crews by the ironic name of 'Happy Valley'. Our bomb load was to be standard, but the weather forecast was not all that promising. Cloud was moving in from the west, which might affect us on our return, but ahead of this, the cloud was said to be well broken so our target should be visible.

I won't go through the preliminaries here, suffice it to say that I tucked myself into 'the tin' once we were airborne and sat back to see what the night would bring. Our route took us out along the line of the Frisian Islands, from whence we would eventually head in a southerly direction for Essen.

From the outset, it was obvious that the Met people had got it wrong, as a solid mass of cloud was clearly visible below and as we progressed eastwards, we saw that the cloud was becoming denser ahead. We pressed on into it but two ominous developments took place: a film of ice appeared on the windscreen and an opaque mass of rime ice began to spread out along the leading edge of each wing. I could not see this, of course, but the conversation from up front showed King's concern. That apart, as we flew along in cloud, we began to pick up turbulence, a sure indication that embedded in this layered cloud were cumulus or maybe even cumulo-nimbus clouds, both giving an increased risk of icing. I did not realise it at the time, but the engines had started rough running as ice found it's way into the fuel inlet system. There was a hurried conference, since it was pretty obvious that the target was unlikely to be identifiable, so the decision was to fly on and see what happened when we reached our ETA (Estimated Time of Arrival).

In the event, at that time, we were still in dense cloud, the whole mass being lit up by searchlights sweeping below, with frequent bright flashes which could have been anti aircraft fire or bomb bursts, I certainly knew not what. With no sight of the ground, and weather conditions totally unsuitable, a decision was made not to bomb, but to seek out some alternative target on the way home. I could follow the general plan, and as we headed homewards, in a more or less direct route, the cloud began to break up to the west, quite the opposite to what the weather man had said. I was upset that I had no part to play in what followed, but I did see the result from my little office in the rear. We did in fact fly along the Scheldte estuary, and as we passed over the port of Flushing, the navigator let go with our total load, and I clearly saw bomb bursts, though I wasn't sure precisely where they landed. This area was pretty well defended, but they had not been expecting us and so by the time they threw everything into the sky, we were well out to sea and I watched the firework display in safety from my vantage point.

It was an uneventful ride home and a smooth landing at Hemswell, followed by the standard air crew breakfast of eggs and bacon, a luxury in wartime. The official report of that raid said that many aircraft had suffered severe icing problems, few had claimed to see the target, and alternatives had been bombed as a result.

I had learned a few things that night. That weathermen could be wrong, that the Rhur could put up formidable opposition, that the enemy could sometimes be caught napping and that it was ruddy cold in the rear end of a Hampden!

It is worth mentioning at this stage, one additional item of equipment that most of our Hampdens carried, namely, the camera. This was on a fixed mounting in the rear of the aeroplane;

the shutter being operated by a flash flare dropped by the crew. Thus, in that sense, it was an automatic system. The flare always went away at or about the same time as the bombs so that, in theory, it should be possible to record the bomb bursts. In fact, I have to confess that although I obtained some good photographs in my time with the Command, bomb bursts were never part of them. That did not mean we had failed in our task, it was merely a question of the timing of the shutter action, and that was out of our hands.

As a challenge, and for a bit of fun, a collection of one shilling per crew-member was made, and the total from all the crews on a raid put into a 'kitty'. The crew with the best target photograph took the pot. If, say, eight aeroplanes operated on a particular night, the winning crew gained the princely sum of thirty-two shillings – eight shillings each. Hardly enough to make us rich but pride was the important aspect of being a winner.

Of course the main reason for the camera was to provide proof that we had found our designated target. Even in the early days of the war, the Germans had perfected the art of laying dummy target areas, sufficiently close to the real thing to trap the unwary. Dummy fires were lit, searchlights and associated anti-aircraft guns were placed nearby, and when all were in action at the same time it was not difficult to be fooled. These searchlights and guns were not wasted, since even on dummy sites they could still be effective. It is a known fact that, until we were made fully aware of the situation, many RAF bombs performed a crude ploughing job on German fields. However, once the wasted efforts became apparent, there was a tightening of procedures, particularly with regard to the identification of the target approach areas, and it was not regarded as a mortal sin to return with one's bombs, having failed to identify, rather than to risk bombing a possible dummy. That apart, there were often alternative targets, both formal or, as sometimes happened, those which for one reason or another happened to be there when you had unused bombs on board, my earlier experience at Flushing being one such example.

Having tucked that semi-abortive raid under my belt, I was informed that I must now join a crew as a permanent member, although, like it or not, I would once again have to serve a stint in 'the tin'.

My new skipper was to be 'Con' Curtis, the navigator Andy Anderson, the Radio man 'Goldie' Goulder and poor old me, for the time-being at least, the under gunner.

I have used the term 'permanent' for that crew but little did we know that what is often known as 'the fickle finger of fate' was to deal us a cruel blow and make sure that this new set up would be far from permanent. What happened would leave me with a scarred memory which lives on to this day. (Incidentally, Goldie and I are still in touch, fifty-eight years after the event which I have yet to describe.)

My first trip with Con was to be to Magdeberg, where having been routed via the Elbe estuary, we were to bomb oil installations with a standard load of four 500lb and two 250lb bombs. But before recording our first adventure together, perhaps a few details of the procedures surrounding each operation would provide a useful background.

CHAPTER SEVEN

The Logistics

We tended to think solely of our own crew or maybe the squadron's effort on any particular occasion, but of course the picture was far broader than that, and a decision to attack a target could well have originated with the Prime Minister. It certainly did later in the war.

Once the target and type of attack had been determined, orders were passed down to the various Group Headquarters, in our case to No 5 Group. HQ having decided on the number of aircraft needed and the appropriate bomb load, squadron commanders were then given their particular requirements. Quite often the bomb loads could vary between aeroplanes in one squadron. They could be a mix of high explosive bombs and incendiaries, or in some cases, with a need to create massive fires, a load consisting entirely of incendiary bombs.

Such information once passed to the Armament Officer enabled his team to contact the bomb dump, at least one being sited on every aerodrome, and to commence loading up the bomb trolleys ready to transport their deadly load out to each aeroplane, as soon as it returned from it's night flying test.

The various specialists in navigation, signals, bombing, gunnery, weather and enemy intelligence assembled and prepared their information ready to impart it to the crews at the subsequent formal briefing.

Station and Squadron Commanders were already fully in the picture, indeed on many occasions, one or both might well take part in the raid. I believe that such decisions did not go down too well with HQ, but it did a lot for our morale to know that the "Guv'nor" was with us on a number of occasions.

Station sick quarters were put on alert in case their services were needed, as were the catering people who would eventually be called upon to prepare the aircrew supper or breakfast. Transport was set up, invariably to be driven by our charming young WAAFs. How could we have done without their support, their care and the efficiency with which they carried out their tasks! They did so much for us all – and I haven't even mentioned the long and short term romances which inevitably developed. (The short term for reasons which will later become evident.)

A flarepath party had to be organised to lay out the goose-neck paraffin flares which defined the take off run and, of course, there was a control caravan sited at the start of the take off run point, wherein someone sat or stood with an Aldis lamp to signal a green light for 'clearance to go' or a red for 'hold' or 'abort'.

A 'Chance light' was also placed at this point and when lit, it illuminated a wide area of one part of the airfield in brilliant white light to assist in the initial stages of the take off run. It was, in effect, the 1940s equivalent of the modern floodlight.

Meanwhile, somewhere else on the unit, a small team was gearing up to tow the 'Pundit' out to its preselected site for that night.

Once confirmation had been received that the raid was positively 'on' crews were provided with 'wakey-wakey' tablets; these were pep pills [amphetamines] designed to stave off tiredness. I stress 'once the raid was confirmed as *on*'. If an operation was called off at the last minute, crew members would find it impossible to obtain any sleep that night if they had previously 'popped the pill'.

I have already explained that briefing procedures were pretty well standardised, but in the event of a major raid the atmosphere and procedure took on a more formal and serious approach.

When the target and a successful result were likely to attract publicity which could be used for maximum propaganda effect, the AOC and his team could well turn up to add emphasis to the need for concentration of effort, although this was not necessary, as, like good Boy Scouts, we always 'did our best'.

Briefing time would be announced on the Tannoy (PA) system, and depending on the chosen time, crew members would either retire to their rooms or congregate in the Mess and perhaps listen to the radio and the melodious voice of a certain young lady named Vera Lynn, singing morale boosting patriotic songs such as *Blue Birds Over....*, *We'll Meet Again* and *When the Lights Go On Again* – and oh how they stirred our young hearts! – especially as we contemplated a mission from which we might not return.

If you were a member of an all NCO crew it was almost for certain that you would congregate together and conversation would drift towards the possible target for that night and tactics which might be employed in the event of any of the various forms of 'trouble' that might be expected.

When I use the word 'trouble' in this context, I am thinking back to some of our tougher targets and the frightening concentration of fire that was aimed at us. This in turn brings back a classic story of typical RAF humour. One particular crew were having an atrocious time over the target, with everything imaginable being thrown at them, ack-ack bursts all around them, trapped by searchlights, shrapnel hammering on the side of the aeroplane, which was being thrown all over the sky. Finally, the Skipper turned to the nearest crew member and said *"Do you think we might have upset them?"*

Any story which tended towards exaggeration or appeared boastful, came under the heading of 'shooting a line' and many squadrons set up a 'line book' in which all such stories were recorded. In almost every case they had a humorous side, and many were invented purely for laughs. Maybe one day, someone will assemble them together and publish them in book form; I reckon it will prove to be a best seller!

Digressing again for a moment, I sometimes wonder what today's generation would make of the conversation if they were suddenly thrust into the company of the young aviators of circa 1940.

Conversation might have consisted of expressions such as 'wizard prang' (a successful raid), "bang on" (great or good), "wacko" (similar to bang on), "sprog" (a new boy or uninitiated crew member), "penguin" (a non-operational person, maybe an education officer), "chiefie" (an NCO, normally in a technical grade), "flat hat" (a Warrant Officer, 1st or 2nd Class, often a strict disciplinarian, who wore an officer-style peaked hat), "nasty do" (self-explanatory, usually referring to a crash), "blood wagon" (ambulance), "Holy Joe" or "Sky Pilot" (the Chaplain), "blackouts" (WAAF Service-issue knickers), "passion killers" (certain other articles of WAAF Service issue clothing), "brown jobs" (Army personnel), "line shooting" (bragging or boasting), "LMF" (Lacking moral fibre, to be explained later), "Brighton B" (A tough course designed to instil discipline into offenders guilty of low flying or similar offences), "undercart" (undercarriage), "knobs and tits" (any form of switch gear) .... and so it went on.

At or about this time 'Pilot Officer Prune' appeared on the scene. This prize 'nerd' was a fictional commissioned officer of the lowest possible rank who managed to foul up almost every task which he undertook. He appeared on a series of safety posters which said *"PO Prune says..."* followed by genuine guidance on what not to do, or more precisely, what to do – and very effective they were too. A number of cartoon-style books were also produced to illustrate his activities, and I'm sure that they are collector's items today.

Intelligence Officers have already been mentioned. Their duty, apart from an input to the formal briefing was to interrogate crews on their return and, as a consequence, build up an unbiased report of the raid and it's probable outcome.

Turning to the Hampden aircraft and its crew, the pilot, to get to his commanding position 'up on top', made his way up onto the port wing, wearing an 'underslung' parachute – which acted as a form of less-than-comfortable cushion – and lowered himself into his seat. He was then confronted with an array of instruments and switches, the most important, in flight, being his so called "blind flying panel" comprising engine instruments, altimeter, airspeed indicator, artificial horizon, rate of climb indicator, directional gyro and, last but not least, a magnetic compass.

The wireless operator/air gunner climbed into an upper hatch entrance and then moved to the rear upper position where his radio gear was positioned, together with the pair of upper guns. The air gunner followed the same route, but then prepared himself for his eventual move into 'the tin'.

Prior to boarding, the navigator, armed with route and weather information, made his way to the crew room where he picked up his canvas navigation bag containing topographical maps, an occasional chart devoid of all but outline features and his navigation instruments. The latter comprised a pair of dividers, a protractor, a straight edge plastic ruler and a 'Dalton Computer'. The Dalton was far from being the type of electronic device we know today; it was, however, a cleverly designed instrument which enabled the navigator to calculate all the necessary values which he needed to perform his task without having to fall back on basic plotting procedures. Armed with this gear and information, the navigator plotted the prescribed route on his map for easy reference in flight, and then set about calculating the necessary compass headings for each sector of the flight, entering them onto a 'flight plan pro forma', again for ready reference in flight in the event of not being able to update wind speed and direction by visual reference once under way. That task completed, the navigator could then join the rest of the crew. Many months later, the arrival of a very primitive form of bubble sextant gave the navigator one additional item of equipment to check.

It is worth mentioning that the only use to which I ever put the sextant was to take shots of the Pole Star on the way home, in order to establish our latitude when little else was available by way of aids, but I understand that the CO of a Whitley squadron claimed to have bombed Bremen after fixing his position by star sights. I have little doubt that this was true, because that same person became a leading light in the post war development of the DH Comet operations, both aircraft and route.

Once ready for departure, the navigator climbed on board using a roof hatch immediately behind the pilot. From this position he had to slide under the pilot's seat and on down into the "glasshouse" in the nose of the aeroplane. Here he unpacked his instruments and other gear, checked the intercommunication link with other crew members and then when all was safely stowed, returned to sit on a small pad directly behind the pilot, and strap himself in with a large sheet of armour plating directly ahead of him, ready for take off. Once the aeroplane had taken to the air, the navigator then returned to his very exposed position in the nose and 'set up his office'. A hinged chart table was swung down from the side, whilst he adjusted his rear end on to small stool-type seat. The position had large black curtaining alongside which could be pulled across to prevent light escaping, and as already mentioned, lighting consisted of red or white miniature angle-poise lamps with rheostat controls to cut light back to a minimum. In this forward position there were just the essential instruments of an airspeed indicator, an altimeter and a small magnetic compass. The bombsight sat prominently in the forward section, while up on the right was the bomb fusing and release gear.

Although not used very often, a forward firing Browning machine gun was fitted just above the navigator's head, and although the pilot controlled the firing of this gun, it was the navigator's duty to cock it when required. Finally, we had radio telegraphy equipment available for communications when radio silence could, or had to be, broken – this was done by the use of a Morse key and Morse code. Radio telephony was available in a limited way, but it was decidedly short range and used between the aircraft and ground control, mostly on return to our base station. It was not unusual for WAAF operators to act as communicators, using a coded call sign. I suspect that the higher pitch of their voices enabled them to be better understood in the very poor reception conditions, which then prevailed.

It should be mentioned that all crew-members other than the pilot wore a kind of canvas half-jacket with metal clips at the front.

Their parachutes were carried as packs, to be clipped to the front of the jacket should the need to bale out arise. Parachute packing was carried out by WAAFs under the direction of an NCO, and we paid occasional visits to the parachute packing section to derive comfort from watching the care with which this operation was carried out. A rubber dinghy was carried on our aeroplanes, normally stowed in the wing for manual release after ditching, should such an unfortunate event occur, and many lives were thereby saved when crews were forced to ditch, usually in the North Sea, as a result of fuel shortage or enemy action. Survivors of a ditching episode became members of the Goldfish Club and were then enabled to proudly wear the emblem of that exclusive club, a winged goldfish.

The other exclusive club was the Caterpillar Club, whose members wore the gold emblem of a silkworm as evidence that they had survived as a result of a successful baling out from an aircraft. If the caterpillar sported red eyes, it indicated that the wearer had baled out from an aircraft which was on fire.

Few people realise that in those days we also had an additional crew-member or two, in the shape of pigeons. If, for example, an aircraft was forced to ditch without being able to send off a distress signal, it was possible to use one of our feathered friends and his homing instinct to notify base of the emergency situation. I believe that there were recorded instances of lives being saved by this method.

Two other items of equipment were 'IFF' and the 'Syko Machine'. The former was a beacon, which, when switched on, identified us as to our own forces as friendly, to prevent them shooting at us – or so we hoped. (IFF = *Identification Friend or Foe*).

The Syko machine was a crude form of encoding/decoding device. It was contained in a metal box, and consisted of columns of letters which could be moved vertically downwards, until a complete word was spelled out at the foot of the display,

A card containing columns of mixed letters, which was changed daily, was placed underneath the display so that as the required letter in each column was moved to the base, abacus style, a coded letter could be read off from the exposed card and the coded word or message then transmitted. Since I never had occasion to use this machine, so I cannot comment on its usefulness, but it seems to have remained standard equipment for quite a while.

In the foregoing, I have attempted to describe the basic crew pre-flight functions, together with the facilities in our particular aircraft, but I still reflect upon the fact that, in the end, everything culminated in the simple process of pressing a spring-loaded switch and uttering the words "bombs gone!"

CHAPTER EIGHT

It Begins in Earnest

A few days after that first raid, I was advised that I had now been rostered with my new crew on a regular basis, the previous navigator having left them for a reason that was never explained to me. So it was that in mid-October I joined the aforementioned Sergeant 'Con' Curtis, and the other two members 'Andy' Anderson and 'Goldie' Goulder, but yet again I would have to fly a couple of introductory trips in the 'tin', after which I would at long last be able to operate in the capacity for which I had been trained, as navigator.

We did not have to wait long, as a day or so later we joined the group at briefing for a raid on the oil installations at Magdeburg, well down the river Elbe, with weather conditions which were favourable in most respects. Favourable because there was sufficient moon to ensure moderately accurate map reading, and part cloud cover, which would give us something to duck into should a night fighter come our way.

We carried the standard bomb load of four 500lb and two 250lb bombs, the latter being on wing racks.

As was normal for most flights to northern Europe, we departed from the English coast at Mablethorpe, heading for the Frisian Islands, which allowed aircraft to stay close to the coast and hence stay clear of too much opposition in the early stages. From my underslung position, I glanced either way and saw one or two aeroplanes heading roughly in the same direction, only to fade into the rapidly darkening sky as the last vestiges of twilight faded in the west. Then came that strange feeling of loneliness with no sound but the steady roar of the engines and an occasional brief word from the pilot over the intercom. This, in the early days, gave us time to think, before things hotted up, and to question just what had led us to embark on this crazy life! Once into enemy territory, the need for vigilance and action, left no time for further thought.

Were we afraid? Of course we were, but it was just 'not done' to admit it. I think that it was the ability to operate under such conditions which made men of boys, although a few, very few, did succumb to their fears.

When circumstances justified fear, even in the bravest, there was no cringing or whingeing, just an outflow of well chosen expletives to vent our feelings for those who gave us greatest cause for concern – "the bleedin' Germans!"

For the few who simply could not cope, there were two options. One was to approach either the Medical Officer or the Padre and endeavour to explain, quite openly, how fear had taken over to the detriment of carrying out safe operations. There was an element of sympathy for such persons, for such a confession required a certain amount of bravery in itself when considering the subsequent opinions which might well emanate from fellow crew members.

Sadly, there was a second group who took what really was the coward's way out – yet some cases still evoked sympathy from their colleagues. One pilot, fearful of enemy action, took it upon himself to fly up and down the North Sea, and dump his bombs in the water. Unfortunately, he forgot to switch his IFF off and hence his action was noted. Not that there was any such thing as a radar plot, but a combination of events eventually led to a confession by his crew and he was Court Martialed, classed as 'LMF' and that was it. In all such cases, the culprit disappeared from the unit almost overnight, and thereafter became the subject of occasional discussion and an example of the penalty for such behaviour.

One thing was for sure; such persons were never rated very highly by anyone from that time forward and were never seen near a squadron again.

To return to the raid, most of what transpired came to me through the intercom system, since, sitting in the 'tin' I tended to see what had happened after the event. Andy reported searchlight and ack-ack activity and used it to establish a rough position from the known areas of defences. Certainly, our run over the target was a trifle hectic, requiring a fair measure of diving and weaving to avoid being coned by the searchlights. Eventually, I heard Andy's quiet voice calling directions on to the aiming point and then the final "bombs gone". It was reasonably clear down below, with broken cloud, and as we banked away I could clearly see flashes in between the sources of the searchlights, which I took to be either gunfire or bomb bursts, though from the timing, I assumed them to be the latter, which hopefully would be confirmed by a successful photograph.

When I reflect upon subsequent raids, I think that this was to be regarded as uneventful, and an extract from official raid records states:

> "134 aircraft bombed many targets in Germany with much of the effort on oil targets. There were no losses on any of these raids and an attack by nine Fairey Battles on Channel ports was the last occasion on which this aircraft operated in Bomber Command".

My next raid was scheduled for October 24th, when the squadron was briefed to attack Hanover and at long last I was to act as navigator.

We departed from Hemswell in twilight and once again, over Mablethorpe, I saw a few Hampdens climbing laboriously up to their cruising altitude, prior to settling down to the long run.

I had given Con a heading for our first check point and I settled down to await the ETA for the Dutch coast, although long before that time I could see searchlights sweeping the sky ahead, accompanied by occasional flashes, presumably where an unsuspecting crew had stumbled across one of the enemy hot spots. We had no problem in skirting the defensive positions and leaving them behind, before taking up a heading for Hanover. At least 20 minutes before our estimated arrival over the target it became obvious that this raid was going give us major problems. A combination of searchlight cones and endless flashes from gunfire and bomb bursts lit up the sky ahead and before we were in a position to identify our target, it was obvious from the mass of red and orange diffused light down below that many large fires were already raging.

Between searchlight beams, it was possible to identify the general target area, but before we eased down a few thousand feet to our agreed bombing height, I had a good look around since we had been warned that the enemy had sited balloons over the city.

Picking out the target, I directed Con onto a final run, whilst he flew the aeroplane porpoise fashion to prevent the master searchlight controller from establishing our track and thereby setting up a cone of searchlights to hold us while the gunners took aim. Off to the left and out of the corner of my eye, I saw a cone of searchlights and there in the centre was a silver cigar-shape brilliantly illuminated, with an orange glow in the centre. Some poor souls had been trapped and one could only pray that the crew would have time to bale out and save themselves.

Looking ahead to the target once more, and noting the comparative quietness since Con had reduced power as we descended, I saw dead ahead and coming up fast, a dense black mass. I screamed "Balloon!" and crouched back as we hurtled straight for it, with no time for avoiding action.

My only thought was 'this is it then, no Hemswell, no family, it will all be over any second now.'

It was all over in an instant, but not as I had anticipated. We went straight into the centre of the balloon – only it wasn't a balloon – it was a shell burst and we had hurtled into the expanding cloud so that I even caught the strange whiff of cordite as we came out the other side. In spite of the glare of searchlights it was still possible to identify the general area, and once Con had pulled us out of the avoiding action which he had somewhat belatedly taken, we levelled off and I confess to then releasing the bombs on to a general, rather than a specific, point. It was of no great significance at this time, because everything seemed to be falling in and around the correct aiming point.

Immediately afterwards, Con made a steep turn to the right, and we headed for home, leaving the others to do their work too. It was then that we realised we still had our two 250lb bombs on the wings. We plodded our way westward through the night with no signs of activity down below, until, as we approached the Dutch coast, we saw the faint lights of an aerodrome flare path where perhaps training or other night flying activity was taking place. It was aligned east/west and so with no indication that those down below were even aware of our presence, we headed in precisely the same direction and, with a textbook run up, I released our two bombs. We saw no evidence of bomb bursts, but whatever else, it gave the Germans one heck of a surprise and as we discovered subsequently, we had in fact bombed De Kooy aerodrome in Holland. In a short time we were out over the North Sea and heading for the Wash and the Lincolnshire coast. There was no more pleasing a sight than the Hemswell pundit flashing in the distance and the thought of eggs and bacon and a warm bed.

I have already mentioned the searchlight system used by the enemy, but just to elaborate a little, I should explain that some form of detection system existed whereby the Germans could hold on to an aircraft, and then, having directed a so called "master beam" onto it, set up a number of others, almost in a circle, the net result being that the lights formed a giant cone in the sky, trapping the aircraft in the centre. It was a comparatively simple matter then, for the gunners to pour everything into the apex of the cone with deadly accuracy. If trapped in such a cone, it was only after violent and often dangerous tactics that one could escape, and it has to be admitted that the odds in such circumstances were usually in the German's favour.

Many times, friends have asked me how I can retain such vivid memories of these incidents. The answer is that my flying log book lists all the raids in which I took part, and after long hours at the Public Records Office at Kew, I have supplemented this information with detail from RAF records, so that a quick glance at a key word, brings back the memories. As an example, the one word 'balloons' against the Hanover entry, is all that I need.

I am often asked also, how the bonding between crew members became so strong, and lasted for so long. My answer is that unless you've been there and survived yourself, you will never understand. Going into a situation where your life could be ended any second, and being together and dependent on each other, simply bonds you as one. I know that I am not over dramatising the situation, for that's how it was, and following an event which I have yet to describe, I am still in regular contact with 'Goldie' Goulder, fifty eight years later, and we still recall, in great detail, all that happened in those far off days.

Walking back to debriefing after the Hanover raid, I little realised that in around 48 hours time, I would live through a period of danger and horror that would leave it's mark on me for all time.

On the night of October 25th, my crew was assigned to take part in a major raid on oil and port installations at Keil, carrying a standard bomb load yet again. Other aircraft were to be in the same area dropping sea mines into the port approaches.

For reasons, which I never discovered, I was once again relegated to the 'tin', but as events turned out, I can only surmise that it was fate which so decreed.

In spite of a favourable forecast, when we arrived over the assumed target area we were in thick cloud and there appeared to be no evidence of attack activity down below. We therefore decided not to waste time in a hopeless search, but to head westwards and deposit our bombs on the fortified island of Borkum. Unfortunately, the cloud persisted, presumably as the result of a weather front moving to the east faster than antici- pated. There was no disgrace in taking bombs back to base, better to do that than just to drop them aimlessly in the sea or through cloud, and so we set off for home, just a little upset at the wasted effort.

The ride home was uneventful and sighting the Hemswell pundit we joined the landing circuit. What struck me as strange at the time was the fact that no voice communication between us and the ground unit was taking place. I found out long afterwards that a German intruder aircraft was overhead and the priority therefore was for the ground crew to set about extinguishing the flare path. I recall a faint line of lights passing slowly beneath us, but I could not understand why Con was not talking to us on the intercom system. Then, as the lights formed part of the flare path, why had we not touched down yet? Still nothing but an eerie silence, not a word from anyone, when I suddenly saw tree tops hurtling by just a matter of feet below me.

It suddenly hit me that we were about to crash.

No time for further thought, there was a tremendous bang, the aeroplane shuddered and as I almost involuntarily drew my legs up. A mass of earth, pieces of metal and sparks flew in all directions as the tin caved in, trapping me above it. We hurtled on, with more juddering and banging until the machine finally shuddered to a halt. Then complete silence, no shouts, and no screams, just emptiness. Looking to the rear I realised that the entire tail section had broken off, but any thought of escaping that way vanished when I saw that the chute holding the camera flares was completely blocking any exit. Looking behind, I spotted Goldie's seemingly lifeless body lying below his position, totally obstructing any movement upwards and outwards that way. I looked again to the rear and to my horror, through the sheared off tail unit, I saw flickering light and heard a strange crackling sound. Right then I learned the meaning of real fear. I was trapped, there was no way out, and the aeroplane was on fire. It was then that I almost vomited with fright when I remembered that the bombs were still on board.

What could I do? I certainly didn't pray. I suppose I instinctively did what anyone would do, I screamed the one word "Help!"

at the top of my voice. The noise of burning was increasing now, and the light of the fire getting brighter, but to make matters worse, as I tried to move, one leg would not respond and I realised that the ankle was broken, at least. I think I was almost on the point of breaking into tears of desperation, when I saw Goldie's body move and I heard a strange voice call "One of 'ems alive!"

I know not how, but that brave soul reached in and managed to ease Goldie up into an almost vertical position and then pull him over the side of the upper gunner's position. I squeezed through into the radio station where, standing on one leg, someone pulled me over the side in like manner. Unfortunately the side of the aeroplane was well and truly ablaze and as I leaned my arm over the side, and in spite of the fact that I was wearing a fur lined leather jacket at the time, the fire burned right through and into my flesh, leaving scars, which I bear to this day. I literally flopped over the side onto the ground and rolled over and over until I finally dropped into a ditch where I passed out. I well recall seeing a murky figure as I came over the side, and I yelled at the top of my voice, "The bloody bombs are still on board!". By this time the aeroplane was a blazing inferno.

At some stage, an ambulance had arrived in the field and despite knowing the risk of exploding bombs its brave crew still came forward to rescue us.

I will relate the follow up incidents later, but the first priority was to get us to hospital, in this case to Lincoln. I say 'us' because, miraculously, we all came out alive. It seems that Con was thrown clear, Andy was shot out ahead and later found wandering some way off, while Goldie and I were rescued by persons unknown.

At Lincoln hospital, dainty and caring nurses and sisters gave their all to see that these poor RAF lads were put into some sort of condition to justify an early move to the RAF hospital at Rauceby a few miles away near Sleaford.

So what did I learn from that night? Well firstly, the sense of real terror and despair when it seems that all is lost. Secondly, that there is always hope, even if it is not immediately apparent. Thirdly, that in conditions of extreme danger, others are sometimes prepared to risk their lives to help save a fellow creature, and finally that perhaps fate does have a part to play in our lives, though of that fact we can never be quite sure.

Many people were involved in that incident on the night of October 25th/26th 1940, some of whom I did eventually meet though in a few instances not until many years later.

At Rauceby, we were placed in a ward where most of the patients were survivors, of one sort or another, from aeroplane accidents and although we felt pretty sorry for ourselves with our injuries, we soon learned that in no way whatsoever did they compare with those suffered by some of the poor souls recovering there. Many were severe burn cases and in due time they were transferred to Sir Archibald McIndoe's establishment at East Grinstead, which was rapidly gearing up to cope with the treatment of such wounds, including pioneer work in skin grafting and plastic surgery.

Some of these poor chaps had hideous facial burns, which would leave them scarred for life, yet the indomitable spirit they displayed was beyond belief. There was simply no time for moaning and groaning in that ward, and there was usually uproar when a new case arrived, particularly if the individual was from a rival squadron. There were shouts to the staff to move the newcomer to another ward set up to deal with this or that particular squadron since, due to complete incompetence, it had more crashes than any other in the Group. All good innocent fun but it helped to keep spirits high. On rare occasions, staff had to fit an 'odd ball' in with us, maybe a hernia or similar problem, and his life became almost unbearable in trying to adjust to the crazy antics and gibes of the 'war wounded'.

The female nursing staff were unbelievably efficient and sympathetic and in our distressed and confined conditions we fell in love with them all. I fell in love with the ward sister, Sister Giles who was pretty, with golden hair piled high on her head, a glorious smile and sweet perfume, the combination of which practically sent me into uncontrollable spasms. Am I exaggerating? Not a bit of it! Although I was very young and impressionable, I still recall that lovely lady with the fondest affection, and I'm nearly in my eighties and hopefully worldly wise, so she must have had something! For that matter, so did all the ladies of Queen Mary's Nursing Service.

Recovery from burns and a breakage took it's time, but unexpectedly, one day, I was dumped at Sleaford Station, with snow falling, to find my way home to Henlow in Bedfordshire, although the RAF did at least remember to give me a travel warrant. Doubtless the hurried departure was caused by a need for bed space to deal with more urgent cases, and as it was time to think about a return to 'work', I didn't complain. The problems of travel with obvious injuries, attracted sympathy and assistance from fellow travellers, particularly as I was then back in uniform, so the journey passed reasonably well. The tears when Mother's poor lad returned injured from the war taught me more about her feelings than I had ever dreamed existed before.

The fact that I still had one leg in plaster and the other in a splint certainly gave greater emphasis to the injury, but I was home, and that was all that mattered for the present. My stay at home lasted for a few weeks, following which I was required to report back for a medical review. In due course the leg plaster was removed, the burns had healed and I was returned to Hemswell for 'light duties'. I had no idea how the great minds at HQ worked in those days, but I was somewhat surprised, to say the least, to hear that I was to be transferred to the other squadron then operating out of Hemswell, No 61, later to become known as the "City of Lincoln" squadron.

In addition, I had already been assigned to a crew, led by Sergeant Peter Sleight, a Grimsby man, with a brash Canadian, Sergeant Burroughs as our gunner and Sergeant Don Pitman as the wireless operator/gunner.

It would be appropriate at this stage, and before leaving 144 Squadron behind, to relate the remarkable follow up to the crash, which did not come to fruition until 1985.

Once the accident had been put behind us, the pace of the war, and my subsequent involvement in aviation for a further 40 years, meant that I hardly ever had occasion to mention the event, and in any case the story held little interest to others as the frequency of serious accidents became horrendous as hostilities progressed.

However, after I retired in 1985, I had a sudden yearning to go back and see if I could discover more of what had happened on that dreadful night. Accordingly, I first wrote to a Lincoln newspaper, related my story and asked them if they could help. Sensing a story, they published details, plus my request, and almost by return the letters began to flow in. The local memorial society offered to set up a visit, with a view to finding the site, and any witnesses.

On the appointed day, I drove to Gainsborough, to be met by a party of enthusiastic ex-service folk and local residents, who promptly took control. In addition to the people who had already written to me, they had contacted others and set up meetings.

It seemed that we had crashed close to a local farm, Cuckoo Farm, and that the farmer himself had been one of the first to arrive on the scene after the crash.

I was contacted by a dear old lady, crippled with arthritis, and then in an old folks home, who remembered being ordered out of her nearby cottage in case the bombs exploded, but had had quite a tussle with authority because she refused to be moved until she had found her purse.

We then made contact with an armourer who still lived in the locality, and who had been ordered out to collect the bombs, which surprisingly enough had never exploded. This was due to the fact that they had been strewn over the crash site, and were not retained in the wreck. He said that, having cleared the site of major wreckage, the smaller pieces of metal were then buried in a huge hole on site.

It was then my good fortune to meet the ebullient farmer, Ernie Till, who just happened to be driving his cattle along a nearby lane, as we drove up. He took us to the precise crash site, for it was on his land that it had all happened. He told how, on hearing the noise and seeing the fire, he had dashed out only to find that his horses had bolted.

Chasing them in the general direction of the fire, he related how he fell over something, and picking himself up, ran like blazes when he saw that it was one of the bombs. I know for a fact that he returned to the site next day, for when I visited his farm years later, I spotted the fire axe, belonging to our aircraft, and no way, up to and including the present day, will he part with that souvenir.

We have been through his story many times since, and it transpired that he was one of those who made a valiant attempt at rescuing us. As proof of this, he had a framed letter from the Station Commander thanking him for his efforts.

Subsequent official enquiries revealed that, in spite of being thrown out, Con had returned in an attempt to save his crew. To this day, I still do not know who it was who finally hauled me up and over the side of that burning aeroplane. Sad to relate, my posting meant that Con and I never met up for any length of time again, and I learned only a few years ago that he had returned to Bomber Command for a second tour of operations and had been shot down in a Lancaster over Paris. This time there were no survivors from his crew.

Many years after leaving the RAF, a group of survivors of the war formed an association whose work eventually led to the completion and dedication of a memorial at Lincoln and I will describe that event later. However, my family attended on that great day, and afterwards we moved on to meet up with Ernie Till, so that they could hear his story at first hand and meet one of the rescuers. The local Historical Society then took us to 'walk' the crash site. I was informed that following annual ploughing, the ground still gave up pieces of metal which could only have originated from our aeroplane. Somewhat reluctantly, one of the members handed over to me a piece of aircraft metal, already identified as part of a Hampden, which I treasure to this day. A very generous gesture, but typical of the good folk of Lincolnshire who have always has a soft spot for the RAF.

Finally, whilst everyone was chatting, I made my way out to that bleak spot in the field and stood silently, just reflecting and musing on what might have been. My family and friends, very thoughtfully, left me that way for a while. On our annual visits to the memorial service, I still make the short journey up to Heapham, and walk quietly out to that spot yet again, and never miss calling on Ernie.

When Goulder had also returned to Hemswell, we approached the Squadron CO and asked if Con could be considered for an award for what we had assumed was a brave rescue attempt. We had no success, and were never given any explanation.

The squadron records simply state:

> *"Oct 25th/26th 1940 Kiel abortive. Five aircraft took off for operational flight. X2998 did not drop bombs and on return to base crashed at Upton, near Hemswell. Crew all injured and taken to Lincoln hospital."*

Many years later we discovered another official entry which said that the crash had been caused by the throttles jamming. On the official side, just a brief entry, but on the personal side, many lifelong memories, some good, some bad.

My future with 61 Squadron started in the B Flight Commander's office where I was formally introduced to Peter Sleight. The first impression was most gratifying, since Peter looked immaculate in his battledress attire and, as I soon learned, this was not just for the occasion; Peter was always smartly dressed, in fact almost the proverbial tailor's dummy, and more importantly his flying matched his attire. There were many occasions in the future when we would appreciate this fact.

Linking with this crew was to be a permanent affair, or as near to permanent as things could be, and we were to be given a short settling in period of local day and night flying before once more embarking on the main task. The thought did occur to me that, after all the fuss and rush to build up the offensive, here I was with just four raids under my belt, over a year after mobilisation.

It was during a short lull that I met up with a wireless operator and we soon became good friends. Together we visited the odd pub or two in Gainsborough where, not surprisingly, we met up with two attractive young WAAFs, thereby forming an ongoing quartet. Doug, my friend, linked up with a blonde young lady known to most of us as 'Biddy' because she operated in the control centre where the radio call sign was 'Biddy'.

My partner was a shy, but very mature lass from Nottingham named Gwen. Gwen was good for me, because apart from being an entertaining partner, she forced me to overcome my occasional immature behaviour and to enjoy what little social life was available to us at that time. When I consider social behaviour today, I marvel at our life then. We visited Gainsborough for a swim now and again, rounded off with a beer or two, and then the ride back to camp in what passed for a bus. Maybe a cuddle and hand holding or squeezing when the opportunity occurred, but little beyond that. Primitive urges were easily curbed without resentment and in spite of all, we were happy. Many months later, when the squadron was required to move south, I realised for the first time just how much Gwen cared for me, when it all poured out in tears, but it was 1940 and life was simple and uncomplicated, albeit sometimes difficult to fathom out.

Anyway, social life, such as it was, had to take second place, and apart from occasional high jinks in the mess, our crew had simply to join the many others and get on with the business of dealing with 'the Hun'.

CHAPTER NINE
Steady and Effective Work

Before settling down – if that is the right word for our routine in those days – with Peter, I did have a short spell of local flying in the Hampden, just to get the feel of things again, although one day, right out of the blue, I became involved with a new giant which had just been flown in to join the squadron, namely the Avro Manchester. This machine, which was the forerunner of the mighty Lancaster, was intended to replace the Hampden on a number of 5 Group units.

Being used to the cramped quarters in our present aeroplanes, we felt that we had moved into another world when we boarded the Manchester. Firstly, it carried a much larger crew, had two power operated gun turrets, a co-pilot, and a strange new character named a Flight Engineer. The flight deck was spacious, by comparison, and the engine power much greater.

However, there was always a price to be paid, and in this instance it was poor engine performance. The twin Vulture engines had a tendency to overheat, and in the event of losing an engine for any one of a whole variety of reasons, the chances of being able to stay in the air for any length of time on the one remaining engine were not good.

The Manchester did go into squadron service and was involved in many major raids, but losses were high and in due course this aeroplane was withdrawn from operational flying, one significant reason being the arrival of the far superior Lancaster.

On one occasion, our squadron commander, Wing Commander Valentine, decided to fly a Manchester on a Berlin raid and, as always, he was accompanied by the various section heads, navigation, gunnery, radio etc. Sad to record, the aircraft and crew failed to return.

Naturally, we were devastated, particularly those who had operated on Hampdens that night and had returned to fly again.

The CO's action was typical of so many of those fine men who led the squadrons and who made sure that they stayed involved as often as circumstances would permit. They never picked a soft target either.

Of course, the work went on, but one never forgot the 'great' men.

A few days after the Manchester introduction, my crew under Peter's leadership, were listed for our first raid together. The main squadron effort that night was on to an inland target in Germany, but, as new boys, we and one other crew were loaded up with a sea mine to be dropped at an offshore point, close by the fortified island of Borkum.

The main stream of aircraft were routed south of the Frisian Islands, but we, being 'loners', were on a roughly parallel route on the seaward side of the islands, so we would need to be alert for any night fighters, seeking out loners or stragglers.

In the circumstances we were left to choose our own route and height and Peter sensibly elected to fly just below a layer of cloud which persisted all the way, and which would provide a safe haven if a fighter aircraft sought to attack us.

From my logbook I see that this really was a "nursery slope" and that the run in was so unbelievably quiet that Peter questioned whether or not I had found the right spot. Fortunately, the enemy cleared up any doubts, for as we let the 'vegetable' go, the shore-based guns opened up and sent streams of tracer our way which, doubtless due to our low altitude, passed well above us. Peter, none the less, followed the usual new boy's post-dropping procedure – he made a 'split-arse' turn onto a westerly heading, poured on the power and headed for the heavens, leaving all troublesome activity behind.

The tracer persisted for a while, and from a comparison of 'drop' times at debriefing, we deduced that this had been directed at our comrades in the other aeroplane. It was a quiet an uneventful ride home and we were in the mess eating our crew breakfast long before the real workers returned that night.

Anxious to absorb our crew into the regular flow, the Flight Commander added our names to the list due to operate on the following night. I recall that, about that time, Burroughs and others had taken to bringing empty bottles and bricks along with them on raids. The latter, when dropped from the 'tin' over the target, gave the air gunners great satisfaction since the bricks were said to have been removed from the rubble of bombed buildings, but I doubt that they did any real harm. The bottles however were said to produce a shrill, howling, sound as they descended thereby adding to the alarm of those on the receiving end down below. I never heard any official confirmation of the said effect, but once again, some satisfaction was gained from adding that little extra nuisance to the night's work.

Anyway, the following afternoon we took off over the Lincolnshire countryside, where, along with others, we went through the necessary checks on aircraft and equipment during the NFT Taxiing in, after our return, we found the armourers waiting with bomb trolleys loaded with 500lb and 250lb bombs.

Briefing took place at a fairly early hour and we learned that our target was to be the docks and oil installations at Hamburg, and once again our outbound track would be along the line of the Frisians.

This was to be a largish raid of some 200 plus aeroplanes, which would include Wellingtons and Manchesters. We would all be heading for the Elbe estuary and thence down to the city. The approach would be a random affair since, as yet, the days of controlled bomber streams had not yet arrived.

We departed just before twilight, after the usual noisy, uncomfortable and disturbing vibration of the aircraft 'bits' as it trundled across the grass until, with sufficient speed, it was hauled into the air, to become our much beloved "mean machine".

Engine controls were reduced to climbing power and we headed for Mablethorpe in the failing light. Over our coastal departure point, I could see, against the last light in the northern sky, a couple of aircraft on roughly the same heading, whilst, silhouetted against the grey background I could just see the shape of one of our 250 pounders suspended below the port wing. It caused me to ponder where it might finish up later that night and likewise what might happen to us.

Night closed in fast, and after a few words on the intercom, all was silent apart from the steady and reassuring roar of the engines.

Yet another brief period in which to reflect on how, why and where, before settling down to my basic navigation checks. Virtually nothing out of routine happened and in due time I picked up the dull outline of the first of the Frisians, putting us pretty well on our required track, comforting indeed.

Flying in piston-engined aeroplanes, air crew who did not have access to engine instruments developed a keen sense of hearing, to the extent that any noise out of the ordinary was often picked up before the instruments signalled trouble. On this occasion, I felt certain that I could hear an irregular beat, but said nothing for fear of being accused of creating alarm. I suppose I should have spoken up earlier, because about half way along the stretch of the islands, the starboard engine started to run rough and then to misfire. Peter went through the prescribed drills involving throttle and mixture but to no avail; to our consternation the airspeed began to fall. Our first full raid as a new crew and this had to happen!

A four-way discussion came to the unanimous conclusion that we should not go on. Due to our reduced airspeed we would arrive over the target long after the others and become a lone target for the gunners, and if the engine were to fail completely, it was doubtful that we could make it all the way home from the target zone.

However, there was no way that we were going to take our bombs back and so we decide to abort from the main raid, and find another target for our bombs. No problem here, for ahead, and to port, we could see searchlights and gunfire originating from Borkum, which although it was not a prescribed target for that night, were obviously using their gunners to shoot at strays and stragglers on their way to points further east.

"That's it!" said Peter "We'll give those bastards on Borkum a hammering!" It was agreed that we would approach on a north-westerly heading and run into the small bay on the south side which, since it was a fortified island, probably had naval install-ations along the shoreline. Of course we had no target map, so everything was done on assumption, but with the volume of opposition coming up from that area, it was safe to assume that the Germans had something to defend down there.

Because the searchlights and gunfire were being directed up to a medium height, Peter decided to descend to well below that level and 'creep' in from an unexpected direction.

For once, things went well, and as we approached the area of activity I could just make out the shoreline with dark masses nearby, and certainly some form of vessels offshore. In the heat of the moment, I forgot the engine, but just for an instant, I heard it cough again. Peter levelled off and said, "OK Timber, it's all yours." I gave him no change of heading, but seeing a dark mass along the sighting bar of the bombsight, having already set the new height thereon, I allowed him to move slowly forward, whilst, still ahead, the enemy were continuing to pump metal skywards.

As the dark mass drifted down to the correct line of sight, I pressed the release button for 'the lot' – bomb bay and wing bombs, hit the jettison bar as an additional safeguard and yelled "Bombs gone!"

Peter threw us into a gut-wrenching tight turn to port and opened up with full climbing power to head across the island and westward for home. The engine did not like this new demand and showed it by thudding and growling like an ancient tractor, but there was nothing we could do about it, as everything was down to Peter from now on.

In the excitement, we had paid little heed to what we had just done, but a yell from the rear brought us quickly back to reality.

"Jesus Christ, look back at what we've done! The bloody place has gone mad!"

Peter's instant response was that there was no way we were going back, but he did make a concession by turning gently to one side, when the reason for the fuss from our gunner became clear. Whether we had hit anything or not could not be determined, but the night sky over the bay was now alight with searchlight cones and shell bursts, plus flashes from the guns, all of which produced a first-class firework display, best seen from a safe distance of course! The gunner claimed that he had seen our bomb bursts but from the enemy's rapid response, and since he may just have detected us coming in, we suspected that it was this and not our bombs which had so fired up our gunner.

"Well, at least we shook the bastards up," said Peter, "Now let's try to get the old girl home."

Very gingerly, the aeroplane was eased up to our agreed cruising height, and once well away from the Frisians, Peter instructed Don to break radio silence and inform Hemswell of our predicament, in case the engine failed completely and we were faced with a ditching in the North Sea.

There was continued rough running, with an occasional cough from the engine, which pushed the pulse rate up somewhat, and with nerves quite definitely on edge, I was most relieved to see the broad sweep of the Wash and, a short while later, the welcoming red light of the Hemswell pundit.

We were debriefed in the normal way, the CO confirming that, in the circumstances, we had made the right decision, and he commended us for our action. Not a very auspicious start to our first bombing raid together, but we needn't have worried, fate would make sure that we got our fair share of the action soon enough.

The engineer's inspection next day revealed that the problem was something he described as 'routine' – points or magneto, I think it was – but it had certainly not been routine for us!

The rest of the squadron returned some two hours or so after us, but regardless of that, a call went out around lunchtime the next day for designated crews to carry out early NFTs, as another raid was on the cards. Following our return from a satisfactory test flight, we noted that once again the bomb loads were standard, ruling out a coastal or naval vessel attack. Briefing was too early to allow much pre-flight rest, indicating a long-range target.

This proved to be so as we were briefed to attack industrial sites and oil installations at Mannheim and Ludwigshaven, both well down the river Rhine and said to be very heavily defended. This flight would be a challenge for me as it was my first really long distance raid as a navigator. However, the targets, fortunately for me, were sited on or near prominent features on the river and we were to have a half moon and part cloud cover most of the time.

Our chosen route was across Norfolk to Aldeburgh, thence over the North Sea to the Schelde estuary, onward to Namur, then direct to the target.

There was an unusually large queue at the take off point, as we had been joined by the 144 boys, and my logbook shows that we were airborne at 22.00 GMT, to begin a slow steady climb to 12,000 feet, at which time the crew commenced using the oxygen supply.

Some distance from the Dutch coast we saw the waiting wall of searchlights, like a line of railings, awaiting the arrival of trespassers. Some of them swept the sky, hoping to pick up an overflying target. Many flashes came from down below as their gunners set about the first insurgents with some vigour. There was always a pretty hot reception in this area, as the Germans had positioned flak ships in the estuary, but we couldn't have had a better indication of our position. We saw no evidence of any aircraft being hit and drew some comfort from the fact that with this much activity from the ground, there was little chance of meeting any night fighters. If the gunfire ceased, it was a sure sign that fighters were about and we needed to be extra vigilant. Much later in the war, tactics changed somewhat, and such assumptions could no longer be made.

We managed to slip through searchlight concentrations, and at the same time, clearly make out the broad sweep of the estuary. It would have been safer to have slipped across the coast further south, but the featureless coastline would have made a visual position check difficult. As it was, we left the coast behind in no doubt as to our position.

Although we had intermittent sight of the ground I could obtain no further reliable visual checks, and for reasons I cannot recall, I did not spot the river Meuse and Namur at the due time. The procedure then was to take up the final planned heading for the target and keep our fingers crossed that we were on course.

Well before our estimated arrival time, we could see activity ahead with several large searchlight cones and frequent diffused light flashes through the broken cloud, so although there was always the possibility of decoy action, there was little doubt on this occasion that we were 'spot on', a fact confirmed in the closing minutes of our run in when easily identifiable loops and curves in the river became clearly visible.

Having no doubt as to the target position, I headed Peter in the general direction as a first step. Things had now begun to hot up, and to one side of us we saw that one poor crew had been trapped in the apex of a cone. We could see shell bursts and tracer all around them, but had little time, or inclination, to devote to them as we had to concentrate on our own problems. Already, the bright fingers of light were sweeping to and fro in our vicinity, while down below, frequent flashes indicated that many of our colleagues were already busy off loading their 'gifts' for the Germans.

No matter how many times one headed in on a bombing run, although one became more accustomed to what was likely to happen, nothing ever really eased the fear or anticipation, however, in spite of the surrounding searchlights and shell bursts, I was able to concentrate on our objective, urged on by Peter to "get my thumb out of my bum" so that we could "drop our lot and eff off home!"

Having already descended to our chosen dropping height, and there being no need for Peter to throw the aeroplane around taking avoiding action, I satisfied myself that I had the correct target, and then with the accepted instructions of "left... left..." or "right a bit", I did my best to ignore all else and directed Peter straight on in. At the precise time of pre set alignment, I pressed the bomb release button and made the announcement the crew had been waiting for, Looking down, I saw what I took to be our camera flash and the gunner was quite certain that he saw our bomb bursts, although the photographic evidence would take care of that, in due course.

Immediately, Peter closed the bomb doors and banked the aircraft steeply to starboard and onto a westerly heading which I would refine more accurately when things had cooled down again.

Approaching the Dutch coast, homeward bound, we could again see much activity from afar, indicating little likelihood of night fighters, but this time we chose to pass to one side, accuracy in fixing our position no longer being vital until we reached the English coast, when we could do so without anyone shooting at us – unless our Royal Navy friends were about!

Descending slowly over the North Sea, we switched on our IFF and in due course picked up the broad sweep of the inlet at Aldeburgh, whereupon we headed for home to pick up at almost the same time, the Hemswell pundit, and just a little ahead, the outline of Lincoln Cathedral, standing proud atop the hill.

My log book shows that 146 aircraft raided Mannheim and Ludwigshaven on that night and the force included Wellington and Whitley squadrons from other Groups, and even a few Manchesters from our own.

Access to German records at a later date showed that this was a particularly successful raid, and our own squadron records, held at Kew, refer to damage to a chemical factory at Mannheim with large accompanying fires, plus damage to 22 light and medium category factories. Not a bad nights work for a bunch of recent schoolboys!

After our safe return, we assumed that we would be in for a short break, but it was not to be. Just 48 hours later we were off to join yet another heavy attack, this time on the docks and the Focke Wulf aircraft factory at Bremen.

Life on this squadron was never going to be dull...

A Hampden of No. 83 Squadron.

CHAPTER TEN

Routine of a Sort

In truth, the only 'routine' aspect of our activities was that we routinely attacked enemy targets. In every other respect it was far from routine: we carried a variety of bomb loads to a wide range of targets in every type of weather and on numerous occasions landed at strange aerodromes – and of course enemy activity could well vary from night to night.

On May 14th 1941, my logbook shows that we carried out an NFT only to find that the planned raid was cancelled due to bad weather over the Continent. This weather was forecast to last for a day or so and we were officially 'stood down' for 48 hours but could not leave the base in case things improved unexpectedly. This gave us a chance to let our hair down for at least one night and so my new-found WAAF friend Gwen and I were able to hold hands and wander to the quieter parts of the camp for a kiss and a cuddle. Good morale boosting stuff!

A weather clearance came along and on May 17th we were airborne on an NFT again. This time, on our return, the armourers reported that they were loading a single 2,000lb bomb per aircraft, plus camera flares, so there was clearly to be 'something special' about the target this time.

Briefing revealed that our target was to be Cologne, and it was planned to put one hundred aircraft over the area in one hour, no mean feat in those days. A plus factor was that it was a moonless night, good news from the safety angle but it would make it more difficulty to identify the target.

It was a late departure that night, 11pm, and once airborne we climbed up into the darkness to finally settle down in inky blackness between layers of cloud, which, it was said, would hold good for best part of the way. I sat in my dark greenhouse, staring ahead into the night, until, as always, the barrier of light and flashes, marking the enemy coast, began to show up as diffused light below the distant cloud. Peter had no problem in gently weaving our aeroplane from side to side, until we had left this activity behind, and then we again settled down on to a steady heading for our target.

Shortly before our ETA for Cologne, intense searchlight activity with well co-ordinated cones left us in little doubt that we had found the right spot. Although the brightness of searchlights against the blackness below made sighting difficult, we had the advantage that the river Rhine was at right angles to our inbound track and as we approached gingerly between lights and flashes, I spotted the clear line of the Rhine, and yelled for Peter to make an instant turn to port so that I could follow this outline. A bridge showed up clearly against the water and having pre-set the bomb sight for all the relevant values, I directed Peter onto what appeared to be jetties and settled us down onto a steady run in. We must have been to the north of the city, because the search-lights and gunfire, whilst still present, were not as intense as those behind us. At the appropriate time, I called for Peter to open the bomb doors, and very shortly after announced that the bomb was on its way. Bomb doors closed, Peter then made the customary hard turn for home, while the gunner reported that he had seen a bright flash on the river bank and felt sure that he had seen our camera flare activate. Our photograph, processed the next day, confirmed damage on the west bank of the river, so we had scored.

The official raid report said that lack of moonlight and intense searchlight activity had made identification of targets difficult, but 82 aircraft claimed good bombing results and industrial buildings were destroyed or damaged. It added that a "well known cafe" and a department store were also hit. There were no aircraft losses that night.

About that time, one facility to aid the navigator on his bombing run had been fitted, but was not well received. The Hampden had a very primitive form of automatic pilot, and an extra miniature control was placed in the navigator's position. It was a small wheel which enabled the navigator to turn the aeroplane left or right on the run in, but the end product, as far as I can recall, was a very flat turn. I suspect that the pilots were very reluctant to relinquish control at such a critical time and certainly, on the one occasion on which I attempted to use it, I found that the attitude changes without the use of conventional controls frightened me. I don't know what happened to this equipment or if it was fitted to many aeroplanes, but it didn't figure in my activities again after that one attempt.

The weather began to turn against us again, and my log book shows two NFTs in the week ahead with cancelled raids to follow, until at the end of that week, we loaded up a sea mine and deposited it into the approaches to the submarine base at St Nazaire. I cannot recall what happened, but we must have hung around for a while, because I see that on the way home, we had to land at Abingdon in Oxfordshire, to top up with fuel before heading for home. The same thing happened two nights later, on the same type of trip, except that this time we called in to uplift extra fuel at Desford (Leicestershire). Mind you, on this occasion there was a very good reason for the long flight, which took eight hours, a long time for our 'flying suitcase'.

As on most minelaying flights, we had been given two 250lb wing bombs, and had thought it prudent not to drop them on the port of St Nazaire. It was too well defended; the submarine pens being under masses of concrete and our tiny bombs could have stirred up a hornet's nest to no good effect.

So we had headed out to the west from St Nazaire, and then turned north across the Brest peninsula heading for a point to the west of Weymouth.

Crossing the landmass, with St Brieuc almost in sight ahead, I was astonished to see, in the blackness below, a brilliantly lit flarepath. I can never understand why, with the noise of our aeroplane close by, and probably others overflying too, no attempt was made to extinguish the lights, but the fact is that they remained on. It could have been a training unit engaged in night flying or maybe a night fighter squadron getting themselves airborne, but it was a chance not to be missed.

We all agreed that we should make the attempt, and Peter, almost as if on a night cross country exercise, made a slow turn on to a reciprocal heading, while down below, there was still no sign of activity of any sort. With the lights now visible to our gunner and well astern, Peter returned to our original heading and the planned target lay dead ahead once more.

I hastily set up the bombsight, and we flew along the line of lights until, without the need for precise accuracy, I pressed the bomb release as the centre of the line of lights came into view. I looked directly below but could see nothing, although the gunner reported flashes to one side of the flare path enabling us to claim a successful strike when we returned to Hemswell. He also added that the lights did eventually go out before the target passed out of sight. I often wonder what it was all about, and whether the delay was in extinguishing flares, or maybe the enemy held on until they had got their fighters airborne. Either way, we saw no opposition of any sort, and it did our spirits a world of good to tackle a target in comparatively quiet conditions, whilst undoubtedly giving someone down below, as Peter so succinctly put it, "a bleedin' good headache." Apart from the refuelling stop already referred to, it was an uneventful ride home to our roost.

Dusseldorf was our target on June 2nd, so we were back to the joys of Happy Valley once more, this time with the standard four plus two-bomb load.

The raid report stated that 150 aircraft took part, but only 107 reported identifying the target, due to adverse weather conditions. German reports state that there was light damage only, but then they would say that wouldn't they? Two Hampdens and one Whitley failed to return.

Much relaxed at our apparent safe return, we were slowly descending over the Wash when, quite unexpectedly, one of the engines started to misfire. The rough running rapidly became worse and Peter decided that he would feather the propeller, shut down the engine and head for the nearest aerodrome. I gave him an immediate heading for Bircham Newton, which was close by, and in the early morning twilight we began to lose height fairly rapidly. Peter had just commenced to turn the aeroplane when that 'fickle finger' prodded us again and the other engine started to misfire too.

We had no option; we would have to go straight down and hope for the best. We were ordered to take up crash positions, so leaving everything as it was, I crawled back under Peter's seat and took up my position directly behind the armour plating at the back of his seat. To this day, I cannot explain why I did not strap myself in with the webbing strap provided – but I didn't – and very shortly afterwards I was to learn the true meaning of 'inertia'.

Looking over Peter's shoulder in the rapidly improving pre-dawn light, I could see that we were heading for a vast expanse of pretty clear agricultural land. Once again, there was no panic, just the awful period of silence I had experienced in my earlier crash. I often wonder if the reason was that each of us was offering up a silent prayer and that this took priority over all else. I suspect that I could be right.

As we closed with the ground, it could be seen to be rushing by at a rapidly increasing rate, until, as Peter pulled off what little power was left and eased the aeroplane into a slightly tail down position, we struck. Noise, dirt, dust, deceleration, all at once, but that was the least of my worries, because on impact, and with no restraint, I shot forward, under Peter's seat, breaking my nose on the armoured plating on the way, before finishing in a crumpled heap in the spot which I had so recently vacated. Fortunately for me, the perspex forward section did not collapse inwards, but not caring very much about that, and with the previous crash fresh in mind, I shot back under Peter's seat yet again determined to be the first out through the roof exit.

Not a chance! As I dropped onto the wing, the radio man was already there and the other two were close behind. I cannot remember the immediate follow-up, because in a matter of less than a minute, a group of khaki clad figures carrying rifles with bayonets fitted, came thundering towards us, the leader yelling "Come on you German bastards, down you come! Watch the buggers lads!"

Who else but our 'friends' the Home Guard doing their duty?

I give Peter full credit, for taking only sufficient time to draw breath, he let go with such a flow of bad language that his nationality was beyond doubt. Almost like a Disney character, their leader skidded to a halt with a rapid, "Sorry Sir, I thought you were bloody Jerries!"

Peter tactfully pointed out the RAF roundels on our aircraft, but when things had quietened down a bit, we had to admit that in the twilight, the shape of our aeroplane could have resembled a German Dornier. However, Peter's great command of the English language had soon resolved the matter!

A local farmer had rushed out to the crash site and after we had convinced him that the damage to his crops, which appeared to be his main concern, was of minor interest to us, he took us back to his farm for mugs of tea while he contacted Swanton Morley, the nearest aerodrome.

They sent an ambulance pretty smartly, and we left the farmer still muttering about compensation. (Oh, how our fellow country-men appreciated us!) Meanwhile our friends in khaki had returned to their barracks, no doubt to relate their own version of the event.

We spent the night in the Station sick quarters while they checked us for shock and/or concussion, but being young and robust we were none the worse for wear. The crash was just another one of those things to be expected from time to time, and next day we were transported back to Hemswell, by which time my swollen nose resembled the front end of a Canadian moose. I found out later that I had broken it.

May I add, somewhat cynically, that no one ever offered us 'counselling', nor have I ever been offered compensation for the spinal and nasal problems which I developed later in life and which have been attributed to that event.

I checked the official report later, and it stated that engine trouble had led to a diversion, but a second engine failure, on approach, led to a forced landing. Crew all safe and uninjured.

A history of 5 Group activities, published after the war, stated that we had, in fact, run out of fuel. At the time, the reason didn't seem important, only our survival, which seems fair enough!

With so many severe injuries being suffered at that time, a chap with a swollen, painful nose could hardly expect sympathy from anyone; indeed one was more likely to become a figure of fun.

"What's the problem mate? Got it caught where it shouldn't have been?" was a typical example.

Fortunately the swelling soon subsided, which was just as well because four days after the crash we found ourselves airborne on yet another NFT.

As had happened before, bad weather over Europe led to a cancellation, and this situation of flight tests followed by cancellations persisted for almost a week. I did manage a quick 48-hour leave pass, which enabled me to rush down to Essex and meet up with some old civilian friends. One evening we headed for a pub in Becontree to listen to a popular, up-and-coming singer named Max Bygraves – and what a pleasurable outing it was listening to his humour and songs. I'll wager that if I met him today and mentioned the Eastbrook pub, he would remember it; he's just that kind of a guy.

After a break of nine days it was back to work again when we were briefed for a minelaying trip in the approaches to Kiel harbour. We had long since come to appreciate that minelaying did not always provide relief from the normal 'shot and shell', particularly when the target areas were close to ports such as Keil, Brest and St Nazaire.

To keep us out of trouble, we were routed to the seaward side of the Frisians, past the fortified base at Sylt, then along what was once the Danish border, after which we headed south into the supposed 'quietest' approach to Kiel.

I use the word 'quietest' in a comparative way, because no approach was ever quiet in the closing stages, and certainly not at Keil.

I have often been asked to describe the appearance of anti-aircraft fire when viewed from an aircraft and find it difficult to isolate from the other factors, such as searchlights, bomb bursts and fires, all of which invariably appeared at the same time. The best comparison I can make is with a firework display viewed from a distance.

First there were the various forms of tracer, which, without considering the calibre of the guns, streamed up into the sky either as broken beads of light forming a steady line, or, if the gunners were 'hosepiping' in the hope of hitting something, as a blanket of staggered lights, mainly white, but occasionally with a colour injected for a reason which I never did discover. Add to that were the heavier calibre shells, which were not evident until they burst, leaving behind a small, expanding cloud of smoke. With searchlight activity, one could often see these "puffs", for want of a better word, flashing by the aircraft like small clouds as we flew on in. No matter how accustomed one became to this type of opposition, nothing could ever remove the fear that the next one might just 'have your name on it'!

To return to the Keil attack... with no moon and part cloud cover we set out across the Danish border when, as we approached the Flensburg area I was surprised to see lights down below. The only explanation that came to mind was that someone down there was trying to provide a clue as to our whereabouts. I thought this terribly brave of the Danes, bearing in mind how the Germans treated such behaviour, and many years after the war I learned from a neighbour, whose mother was Danish, that this was precisely what had been happening. Just one example of how, in spite of German occupation, we still had friends in Europe willing to offer what little help was possible.

The drop was not uneventful; the flak ships did their best to punish us, but pumped most of their ammunition above us on our low-level approach, thank goodness.

The pace now began to quicken, and we carried out four raids in the week or so, which followed. Two were to Cologne, but then came our first attempt to sink the *Tirpitz*, which was still skulking in Keil harbour. However it seemed that whenever we had a chance to take on a raid of some significance, things never quite worked out right.

Having carried out the routine pre-raid tests, we were loaded up with a single 2,000lb armour-piercing bomb, and briefed that our target was that mighty vessel, moored alongside the dock area. However, the weatherman was a little vague about cloud conditions, saying that it might just be building up over the target area for our arrival.

We followed the usual route in, and approaching Kiel from the north could see much activity ahead, but since most of the light was diffused it followed that there was a fair measure of cloud about.

I picked up the coastline with some difficulty but there was little doubt about the target area. One massive cone of search-lights had formed up through a large break in the cloud, and following the path of tracer up into the apex I could clearly distinguish the bright shape of one unfortunate aircraft trapped at the core. There was no time to dwell on his problem, but he was obviously in real trouble.

Keeping the coast to our left, we agreed on our bombing height so I was able to set up the bombsight, for it needed to be accurate with such a small target. The cloud cover was intermittent, and we agreed that whether we sighted the ship or not, we would aim for the dock area, basing the release time on any positive visual fix in the closing stages of the final approach.

Things began to hot up, although most of the searchlight activity seemed to be off to our right, but as we closed in, I spotted numerous dark shapes flashing by either side, above and below, and kept my fingers crossed that they were decaying shell bursts and not balloons. The dock area, highlighted by the activity down below, appeared and disappeared with the gaps in cloud cover, so that I had a reasonable idea of the release point, but I must confess that, with the sudden increase in gunfire and searchlights and the need to avoid an overshoot and the possibility of going around again, I had decided on the precise point at which I would release the bomb. Peter had already opened the bomb doors, and just as the dock site passed beneath cloud, I pressed the button, and with a slight judder from the aeroplane, away went our bomb.

A moment or two later, the under gunner reported a bright flash, which we hoped was our camera flare going off, but with the broken cloud between us and the docks, who was to say. There was no way that we could claim a positive sighting or hit, but we were not alone, since the official report stated: "115 aircraft took part in the raid and met flak in all directions. Very few crews saw the *Tirpitz*; hence bombing was concentrated on the city. A number of the new Stirlings and Halifaxes took part in the raid and two Wellingtons failed to return."

It was not until some time later that the RAF finally caught the *Tirpitz* hiding in Norway, and 'gave it the treatment'.

Another short spell of leave followed and yet again I took myself off to the east end of London to link up with relatives once more. This time I could walk tall, because I knew that I was part of the real fight back, and I lapped up all the attention, bordering on adoration, from some of my young female acquaintances.

I had very strong feelings about the efforts being made by the RAF at that time, particularly when I thought of friends already gone forever. This came home to me very forcibly during my leave when, returning home from a local pub with the family, one member of a group of youngsters standing outside, called out, in sneering fashion, "They fly by night" (the title of a well-known newsreel film about Bomber Command being shown in cinemas at the time).

In an instant, I struck him across the face with my left hand and followed up with a good hard thump to his stomach with my right fist this from a fellow who previously would not have said 'boo' to a goose! Almost at once, I regretted my action, suspecting that the guy might now set about me, but not a bit of it. Looking decidedly ashamed of himself, he said "Sorry mate, it was only a joke." I wondered afterwards if his contrition was due to my actions or to the aggressive stance taken up by my uncle, who had slaved for years in the asphalt business and had hands which looked as though he used them to spread the stuff. I shall never know, but the matter was quickly resolved and we went on our way. However, this incident did indicate how deeply I had been affected by all that was going on at Hemswell and elsewhere, and maybe that young buck gained a better appreciation too.

I called on my mother, but this was a quiet affair, since my sister was serving with the Womens Land Army and my dear old Dad was away with the RAF. He was serving on one of the early aircraft carriers, supervising the assembly of crated Hurricanes which were eventually flown off to a point in West Africa, whence they were flown across the Sahara and up into the Suez canal zone, ready for operational use.

We had a day or so to spare, on return to Hemswell, so Doug and I managed to induce Gwen and Biddy to 'arrange' some time off, which was spent mainly in the city of Lincoln, winding up eventually at the Monk's Arms at Caenby Corner, just a short distance down the road from Hemswell. That much-used pub still exists today, and I often wonder, should I ever call there on our occasional visits up north, if I would find any of the old regulars from way back, who could sit and chat about those hard old days.

CHAPTER ELEVEN

Dare I Look Ahead?

As a crew we had now reached the stage where, having survived a fair number of raids, we were almost becoming veterans, and even risked talking about the chances of completing our allotted number, which still remained as 'about 30' sorties or 200 of hours operational flying. It was evident that a number of our colleagues had already achieved this target and were due for a rest.

Choices were rather strange. Some brave souls opted to continue, but unless there was a good reason from the official angle, they had to stand down. Others, depending on their category, chose to join OTUs (Operational Training Units), where they would pass on their knowledge by flying with new crews who were fast approaching operational status.

Several, like myself, decided that, if fate, or whatever, allowed them to complete their tour, they wished to become instructors at basic training units. Still reluctant to look too far ahead and maybe tempt fate, I nonetheless added my name to the list of potential instructors.

Life, such as it was, rolled on with strange inexplicable events. For example, our crew, along with two others, was ordered to carry out a series of daylight cross-country flights, flying in close formation throughout, with no explanation of the reason. Rumours abounded, mainly conjecturing that we had been specially selected for an important daylight raid on a target yet to be announced.

Opposite page: Hampdens in formation.

Typically, in the midst of all this rumour and worry we were informed that we were to join the squadron that night for a raid on Bremen ... and that was the last we heard of daylight formation flying. One day I'll call at the PRO at Kew and find out what it was all about ... maybe.

Our bomb load for the Bremen raid included two canisters of incendiary bombs, so it looked as if we were on a big 'burning job'. We had grown accustomed to the almost standard route to reach targets in the northern parts of Germany. This time, we had to make a right turn once reaching the mouth of the Weser, down the heavily guarded estuary and on towards Bremen. My log book gives no indication of the result of our effort, but records state that in spite of cloud and haze, good bombing results were obtained, although two Wellingtons and one Hampden failed to return.

As I have written elsewhere, I have to mention a strange effect, which I suffered many times, particularly when I later moved on to civil aviation, known as 'disorientation' – although during my time in Bomber Command it was hardly mentioned as such.

When flying in daylight with a visible horizon, one can be in no doubt as to the aeroplane's attitude. In time, a pilot trained to use what were then known as 'blind flying instruments' learned to rely upon them even when he had no visible horizon, as at night. However, in turbulence, or when making certain man-oeuvres, 'G' forces exerted upon the body can give the impression, as for example in a badly-executed turn, that one is slipping sideways and downwards. Likewise, when flying between two layers of cloud whose outlines do not parallel the true horizon, it is possible, even when instruments show the aircraft to be level, to feel that because the cloud is slightly angled, the aircraft must be tilted to one side also.

Overcoming the evidence of one's own senses is extremely difficult, especially for one such as myself, positioned up front, with no instruments to clarify the situation. It sounds crazy, but it's true. This strange effect first came home to me during that Bremen raid, but I also experienced it on others later on, when the aeroplane, surrounded by and blinded by searchlights, was put into 'non-standard' attitudes when various forces came into play, giving the impression that we were falling out of the sky, or standing on one wing tip, and I feel no shame in confessing that I often hung onto anything close by to avoid falling when, as became evident, no such action was necessary. Anyway, no one else could see me, and who knows what the two gunners were feeling or doing at that time. It is for sure that we never discussed the subject. In due course, I became a little more accustomed to the effect, but could never quite cure myself of the feeling of apprehension.

We were promised a short stand-down after Bremen but, lucky me, I was informed that Sergeant Baker's navigator had been taken ill, and I would have to replace him on a mine laying trip to St Nazaire that night. With no trade union to run to, I just had to grin and bear it, although everyone was superstitious about linking up with strangers at short notice.

At the time there was a need to step up minelaying trips due to increased submarine activity out of the channel ports, and they could not afford to stand down even one aeroplane due to crew sickness.

I see from my records that we were airborne at around 11pm and headed off to the west of London, towards Dorset. Over Chessil beach, one of the engines began to make extremely unhealthy sounds and the instruments indicated trouble. There was nothing to be done but to turn back and head for home with the mine still on board. No problem landing with this beast still attached. We were back, within three hours of departure, digesting our aircrew breakfast long before the rest of the squadron returned, all unharmed on this occasion, thank goodness.

This stroke of good fortune, as I saw it, meant that I could return to my own crew once more, for to be truthful, I felt lost without them, which emphasises what I have already said about bonding.

Once again, we had a break before returning to operational flying, this time for a period of nine days which, while we could not plan what to do, at least enabled us to meet up with the girls once they were off duty. It was during one of these meetings that Gwen said something rather strange to me.

"I don't know what we are going to do when you all move off."

I assumed that she was referring to the great day when our tour would be completed, but not so. The 'scuttlebutt' amongst the WAAFs in the operations section suggested that the whole unit was shortly to depart, but it was only rumour thus far.

There was no time to follow up this whisper since, on July 14th, and back with Peter and the lads again, we were briefed for a raid on Hanover. Laden with a single 1,900lb bomb plus the usual extras on the wings and a camera we were able to carry out a textbook run and achieve good confirmed results. Official reports state that 44 Hampdens joined other aircraft types making a total of 85, many fires were started, crews reporting that the fires could still be seen at a distance long after leaving the target. A fair night's work again.

On our return, the CO was there to greet each and every one of us to impart the news, before we went off to bed, that both squadrons had been ordered to move south, allowing two Polish (I think) Wellington squadrons to move into Hemswell.

The move was to be accomplished in a matter of days, which meant that Doug and I hardly had time to give proper attention to Gwen and Biddy. For my part, it was all rather emotional and certainly very tearful, although it was obvious that the rumour, now fact, had partly prepared the young ladies for the inevitable break. They, of course, being part of the Station staff, would remain and carry on the same work, although how Biddy would cope with communications with the Poles was another problem.

I suppose that Gwen and I must have pledged eternal love and friendship in those last few days together, but after I left I never met up with her again, and the letters which came thick and fast at first, soon dwindled away to nothing. For many years afterwards I did retain a portrait photograph of Gwen, inscribed "to the greatest guy in the world" but I was never sure whether it was vanity alone which caused me to hang on to it.

The bulk of essential stores and ground staff having departed by road, crews loaded up their aeroplanes and headed for Rutland. Our main base was to be at North Luffenham, where all squadron personnel were to be accommodated but, whereas 144 Squadron aircraft were to remain at Luffenham, 61 Squadron machines were to be based at the satellite aerodrome, Woolfox Lodge, a few miles to the east. In fact this small field still exists today and can be seen alongside the A1 just north of Stamford.

The site had most of the essential buildings and runways of a sort, with the grass space in between filled in with logs as a deterrent against possible landings by German gliders, should an invasion ever take place. The main snag was that all formal administration took place at Luffenham and we then had to sit in the back of a truck to be transported to Woolfox for every raid.

After the warmth of welcome accorded to us wherever we went in Lincolnshire, we were somewhat disappointed at our reception in Stamford. During our short settling-in period, we ventured into the town, but it seemed bleak and almost deserted, and the pubs weren't much better. The only real welcome came from the local fire station staff. As so often happened, we found that having settled down to a steady evening's drinking, by the time the landlord had rung the closing bell, the last official transport back to base had departed and being a little too 'under the weather' to walk and not having the means to pay for accommodation, one bright spark discovered that the fire station had spare bunks. It didn't take long to sort out a working arrangement and thereafter, if we did miss the transport, we knew just where a warm welcome awaited us.

I suppose that, as we were a friendly bunch, and the locals began to appreciate just what we were about with our frequent night departures and early morning returns, they began to warm to us and a far better overall atmosphere developed.

Shortly after our arrival, Peter was promoted to Flight Sergeant, which justified a special night of celebration in Stamford, but all too soon we had to settle down to the business of 'taking the war to the Hun' again.

At about this time an incident occurred which, for a brief moment, caused me to question what I was doing in this life of more than just a little danger. Following briefing, we were always transported across to Woolfox by truck, where our aeroplanes and ground crews were standing-by, ready for the night's work. On our way across, one evening, I was sitting in the rear of the Bedford truck when, glancing back as we passed a farm gate at the entrance to a field, I spotted a young man, only partially clad, engaged in what could only be described as an attempt to impregnate the young lady beneath him.

Several others had caught sight of him too, and the quiet of the evening was shattered by raucous yells of encouragement from our group in the back of the truck, which for the short space of time in which the lucky lad was visible, did not seem to affect his performance in the slightest. We moved on, but when things returned to normal, I could not help wondering why I was about to venture out, possibly never to return, whilst our man in the field would soon return to a comfortable bed, fully satisfied in every respect, and be around to repeat his activities on the morrow. It made me feel pretty depressed, rather than jealous, but as any ex-aircrew man will know, when surrounded by good chums, it was difficult not to be cheerful, so the mood soon passed.

I do recall that in the midst of the banter that went on during this event, including such remarks as: "Lucky sod!" and "Go on boy, give it stick!" Peter had made some remark to the effect that he would soon be likewise engaged. Persistent questioning produced the news that he only had a few trips remaining before he completed his 'tour'. We understood his reluctance to say too much, since we were all very superstitious, and any hopeful anticipation on his part would have been seen as 'tempting fate'.

For the rest of us, Peter's safe departure, which we fervently hoped for, would mean our starting all over again with a new skipper, and perhaps not such an efficient one. However, at least for the present, we were still all together.

CHAPTER TWELVE

Light at the End of the Tunnel

To retrace my steps a little, our first outing from Woolfox was a minelaying venture to drop a 'vegetable' in the mouth of the Weser river just short of the marine base at Bremerhaven, as part of the plan to bottle up as much shipping as possible. In addition, we were given the usual 250 pounders on each wing, to play with as circumstances allowed.

Once again, we followed our well-ploughed furrow to the north of the Frisians, comforted by the thought that the various types of activity we could see were well to the south, where presumably less-than-attentive navigators had led their skippers off the main track and over mainland defences

We descended at my estimated time towards the drop area, whereupon Peter questioned the accuracy of my navigation, since it was unbelievably quiet, whereas further ahead there was much searchlight and anti-aircraft activity. I managed to convince Peter that this undoubtedly originated from Bremen or Bremerhaven, which perhaps were also designated targets or had opened up on strays. For my part, I was quite happy that we were in the right spot and so descending down to a few hundred feet, Peter eased back to the required speed and away went the mine.

We did not hang around, but blessed our good fortune and climbed slowly back to our operating height and headed for the reciprocal 'Frisian Islands track' once more.

Just off one of the islands – I can't remember which – we spotted a small vessel, stationary in the line of breaking waves on the north shore. There were no signs of life whatsoever, but remembering our wing bombs, Peter decided that, come what may, we would pop them onto, or about, that ship.

We made a slow wide turn to the north whilst at the same time descending once more to a low level. There was still no sign of life below, and knowing that we could not use our bomb sight for a low level approach, Peter said that he would run along the fore and aft line of the vessel, leaving me to release the bombs on estimate (low-level bombsights did exist at that time, but our aircraft was not fitted with one).

Turning slowly back onto our original heading, and now down to less than a thousand feet, Peter asked me to cock the forward firing Browning machine gun positioned just above my head, and I dutifully obeyed.

Ahead, in the half-light, I could see the outline of the vessel, and as our speed had now built up, it was fast approaching. Bearing in mind our agreed procedure I grabbed the bomb release button, poised ready to press, and just as the shape appeared close ahead, Peter let out a blood curdling scream and pressed the firing mechanism. The noise nearly frightened me out of my skin, as I saw a stream of tracer pour into the ship, and almost without thinking, I pressed the bomb release button and away they went. I certainly never saw any bomb bursts, and the under gunner, who had also decided to let go with fire from his two guns, added that he had seen no bursts either, which was rather strange. Completely fired up, like an overexcited schoolboy, and still yelling profanities at the Third Reich, Peter opened up the throttles and headed for the sky, having decided that to go back for a "look see" might have exposed us to some evil Hun waiting to take revenge. In the event, all behind us remained quiet, which gave the impression that perhaps we had just bombed a beached vessel (on our return, our intelligence people could find no information on there being a ship of any importance in the area, which tended to support this theory).

We had a very quiet ride home again, but for a while the adrenaline had flowed good and fast and we were all totally fired up, which made the whole trip something a little different, and certainly provided a good safe introduction to our remaining time yet to come with Bomber Command.

A few nights later, we were off to Keil once more, and just as apprehensive as always at visiting this hot spot.

I well remember this raid because circumstances permitted us a clear view of the dock area and, having gained more experience, we had by now become far more determined in our attacks. This raid is best summed up by an extract from the squadron's record book:

> "61 Squadron. Flight Sergeant Sleight's crew made two runs at the target, taking two excellent photographs of the dock area, in close proximity to the target area. The rear gunner reported seeing a large fire which remained visible up to forty miles from the target."

I reckon we earned our keep that night!

In the early autumn of 1941, another strange requirement came my way. Without explanation I was given a travel warrant and ordered to report to the Royal Aircraft Research Establishment at Farnborough, where on arrival I was whistled across, with other somewhat bemused airmen to the section which operated the high altitude pressure chamber.

With a little thought, I could have put two and two together, but thus far I hadn't. For some time, there had been rumours that the RAF was to receive a small number of B17 (Flying Fortress) aircraft, with a view to setting up a squadron. Added to this, a few weeks before the visit to Farnborough, we had flown north to Polebrook to take our CO there for some sort of official meeting, details of which were 'not for us to know'. While we were waiting around, we learned from general chitchat that this was the probable home-to-be of the new squadron.

It suddenly dawned on me that the reason for the Farnborough trip was to test our suitability for high level flight, and indeed this was so. Since I never became qualified, I do not know whether the B17 was pressurised or not, but what was certain was that it flew at extremely high altitudes. Anyway, back to the tests.

We were briefed that we would be locked into the chamber and that the pressure inside would be lowered to simulate the rarefied atmosphere aloft. We would then be given a series of mental and physical tests, with and without oxygen, to assess our ability to cope with both sets of conditions, which could well apply when flying in the B17.

In my small group, there was one character who obviously had foreknowledge of the ultimate reason for the tests, and had made up his mind that, no way, did he ever want to fly in this new beast. At the start of our first test, the Medical Officer said that once sealed in, we would be taken up to high altitude and then asked to remove our oxygen masks to note reaction. The large circular door was then closed followed by much hissing and clanging as presumably the airtight seals were made.

There was a steady humming noise with occasional sounds of air entering or escaping air, but I felt no physical changes whatsoever and there was no voice input from the medics outside, although one could just see movement through the porthole windows. Part of our briefing had included the effect of 'bends' as experienced by divers when subjected to rapid changes of pressure, but I was astonished to see that the reluctant crew member sitting opposite me was already writhing in agony, clasping his stomach.

A panic call to the outside produced an almost instant opening of the entrance hatch and this chap was quickly removed. We were then advised that the exercise would get under way immediately, as indeed it did. At some unknown height we were required to carry out calculations and answer questions, whilst receiving a steady oxygen supply. We were then instructed to remove the oxygen masks and after a short time to go through similar exercises. The changes were quite remarkable and brought home the reason for previous warnings about the dangers of oxygen starvation. In addition to the poor test results, we quickly learned that when deprived of oxygen one's reaction times can increase until they become almost non-existent.

In due course we were 'brought down' and fully debriefed, but with no assessment of our overall performance. That would follow later. It was at this stage that we learned the fate of our reluctant colleague.

The doctors were highly amused at his antics, because at the time that he was writhing in agony, the exercise had not even started and the pressure inside the chamber was still normal. They gave him full marks for performance and I am sure that their explanation brought about a full confession of his guilt and they sent him on his way with an assurance that under no circumstances would they post a chap with that attitude to the proposed high-altitude squadron.

The rest of us were returned to our respective units without a clue as to our formal assessment, and I heard no more, although in due course the B17 did indeed go into squadron service under RAF colours.

Around this time, night raids on our cities were building up and the RAF were required to set up night patrols using the Boulton/Paul Defiant aircraft which had a power-operated gun turret. I don't think they had much success, so in due course someone at Air Ministry hit upon a bright idea. Small panels were cut out of the Hampden fuselage in an over wing position and a Vickers gun fitted thereto. The general idea was that we would patrol at night and hopefully shoot down intruders if we saw them before they saw us. In addition, a small single gun was fitted facing forward in the navigator's position, free to swing in an arc. This didn't last long, probably, I always suspected, because some over enthusiastic navigator shot bits off his own aeroplane. Pure supposition, but anything was possible.

Our crew only took part in one such patrol during which we flew around for hours and saw nothing but had a few shots fired at us by the boys down below. I have no idea how long this experiment lasted, but we were never involved again, and all of us thought it a waste of time and manpower.

I still recall a Canadian pilot, I think his surname was Dees, who had been involved in this strange interlude, showing his disgust in a practical way, and thereby coming close to a Court Martial. Returning home after a non eventful patrol, he hurtled in over Woolfox at what we all regarded as 'zero feet', so low that he almost struck the logs strewn around the grass, making several tight turns as he lined up for further runs. It was unexpected, entertaining, and cheered on by all present, except the CO. All it lacked was a victory roll, but discretion won the day. It is for sure that safety didn't.

Pilots were too precious a commodity to haul off from squadrons for anything but the gravest of sins, and after a severe reprimand Dees carried on – a wiser but happier man.

I see that on August 6th we took a standard bomb load to Karlsruhe, and while I cannot recall any details, the records show that we went in low:

> "Flight Sergeant Sleight's crew attacked from 6000 feet and three bomb bursts were observed."

It was also noted that we experienced severe icing conditions on the way home, making the airspeed indicator pretty well inoperative until we finally came down into the aerodrome circuit and warmer temperatures. Not a very pleasant experience, I can assure you.

On the 8th, back to Keil, where anti-aircraft measures were becoming even more intense, but against that, there was a vast improvement in our determination to achieve good bombing results. In essence, the war was really beginning to hot up now.

We carried four 500lb bombs plus two containers of incendiaries, and with a change for the better, as far as weather conditions were concerned. Everyone managed to locate their target and obtain satisfactory results. An added feature was a marked increase in night fighter activity, usually on the homeward route where the Luftwaffe were waiting to pounce on the tired and unwary. Little did we realise that in a day or so, we were to become victims of such a trap.

Three nights later and, just for a change, we were sent off to bomb the railway yards and a parachute-manufacturing factory at Krefeld, which sits halfway between the Dutch border and the river Rhine. We were warned to be particularly careful in determining our position in the closing stages, as any overshoot could take us into the Rhur, in the region of Dusseldorf and Duisburg, where we would get a far warmer welcome than at Krefeld. Being a comparatively short flight of around five hours or so, we did not depart from Woolfox until around midnight, meaning that we started out feeling a little weary.

Routed out over the Schelde estuary, we had no problem in obtaining a position check at the enemy coast since part of the Group had been detailed to attack the docks at Rotterdam, and their presence, coupled with the response from down below, was as good as a road sign. Peter weaved us gently through the local concentrations and then we headed for the target, where on our ETA, cloud cover nearly caused us to abort, but the sweeping searchlights, diffused by the cloud, and intermittent flashes, indicated that we were in the right area. We were not alone in bombing on estimate that night and the official report confirmed that unforecast cloud cover had prevented accurate bombing and only one aeroplane had reported bombing the railway yards.

The ride home, must have been uneventful, since my logbook contains no additional comment.

To our surprise, shortly after surfacing next day, we were ordered to carry out a NFT, as the squadron was to form part of a maximum effort on Magdeburg and Hanover that night. Our crew's contribution was to be one 1,000lb bomb and two 500 pounders, destined for Magdeburg on the Elbe and not that far from Berlin, so this was going to be a long one.

We weren't exactly feeling over the moon at this prospect, added to which, Peter confirmed that this was to be his last trip before being rested.

Having survived thus far, an outsider would have said that he was 'home and dry', and even the ground crew, bless their hearts, pulled his leg unmercifully. But amongst the rest of the aircrew there was much superstitious apprehension that this trip could be Peter's last in a more ominous way – and it very nearly was...

For the rest of us, even if the good Lord of all aviators allowed him to survive, we would still have the problem of flying with a new skipper who might well fall short of Peter's standard (although, in the event, for my part, I finished up with one of the best).

I hesitate to mention it yet again, but we were on 'the Frisian track' once more, until in due time we altered heading down between the two major estuaries, with masses of enemy activity all around, presumably as the Command were giving Bremen, Bremerhaven and Hamburg a good pounding that night.

It was around this point that I saw at first hand a decoy fire in action. I had no doubt of our position, but down below, obviously well away from any town or industrial site, was a large fire, a few searchlights sweeping the sky and an occasional bright flash.

There was no doubt that some unsuspecting soul, not too sure of his position, might be tempted to have a go, and thereby save Fritz a good deal of ploughing time later on.

Conditions were such that we spotted activity around the target from some distance off and had no difficulty in identifying the target area. Our run in was beset with the usual attempts to shoot us out of the sky, but being mindful of Peter's immediate future I headed him in through a comparatively quiet spot, while he, for the same reason, once I had yelled "bombs gone" threw the plane into a steep right hand turn and onto a westerly heading for home. We had made a conscientious attempt at accuracy, and reports confirmed that the fires which we had seen and bombed, were indeed in the target area.

Following the reciprocal route back, we could see that the 'firework displays' to the north were still well under way, so Bomber Command was handing out headaches in full measure that night. Once more we were flying homeward along the seaward side of the islands, thinking of the future and giving Peter a hard time for deserting us when we needed him.

Then it happened... A smart young Luftwaffe guy had obviously been sitting there, just as we had been warned, and found us completely off guard. I heard, above the noise of the engines, the sound of machine gun fire, too slow to be a normal type and most probably a cannon, followed by tracer which came from astern and whistled across the port wing inboard of the engine, while at the same time I heard the upper gunner yell "Fighter!"

My stomach hit my throat as Peter pointed the aeroplane almost vertically downwards and headed for the deck, whilst it seemed that the three of us were all shouting instructions to him which he completely ignored. Just as suddenly, it all became quiet again, no shouting, no gunfire, just a dark mass of water below coming towards us at a rapid rate. Pulling hard on the control column, subjecting us all to a massive G force, Peter slowly pulled the machine back to level flight again.

No attempt was made to climb back up as yet, we just chatted together while taking stock of the situation. It seemed to us that the enemy plane could not have been following us, since neither of the gunners had seen him. It looked as if we had just strayed into his patch and he had taken a shot at us in the hope of a quick kill.

The upper gunner insisted that he had seen tracer bullets coming from ahead and passing astern. At debriefing the intelligence officer suggested that it was probably a JU88, currently being used as a night fighter, which had come in firing forward guns leaving his gunner to fire off astern as he passed us by.

I still cannot recall why, but on this occasion we landed at Wyton, in Huntingdonshire, and dropped in to the Mess for a short rest before carrying on to Hemswell. My brother-in-law, an aircraft fitter, was based at Wyton, and so as soon as we had breakfasted, I found his barrack block and invited him to come along and take a look at our 'bomber'.

Wandering around, he glanced up at the port wing and said "What's all this for then?" Following his upraised arm, you could have knocked me over with the proverbial feather for there along the port wing, inboard of the engine, was a line of deep gashes, the end product of the enemy fighter's gunfire.

I confess that a dreadful icy feeling hit the base of my stomach, not from the sight of the damage, but from the instant thought that we had come as close to being shot down as one can get, yet had still got away with it, and on Peter's last raid, at that!

I contacted him immediately and he came along with the Station Engineer, who having first phoned Hemswell, announced that we would be allowed to fly back, but only with minimum fuel and minus any surplus gear in order to keep the aeroplane as light as possible.

Having flown back from the raid we were not unduly worried by the short hop up to our base, but the audible sighs of relief and yells of delight from Peter as the old girl was 'greased' onto the surface raised our spirits tremendously.

We had one very happy pilot on our hands, and following a period of afternoon rest, we celebrated in the time-honoured fashion of attempting to drink the Monk's Arms dry. At that time we gave little thought to our immediate future, but I did take stock on the following day.

By my reckoning, I had three more trips to complete before I could join the fortunate elite and stand down for a while. There was little time wasting and I was duly informed that I was to join Flight Lieutenant Casement's crew and serve my time out with him.

This officer was an efficient and determined man, who went on to receive decorations for bravery during his service, including, I was told, an occasion when he put paid to a German U-boat.

I found him to be extremely calm under stress and he thought nothing of holding off from a target until it had been positively identified, and then returning after having bombed to take a look at the general damage.

I should mention that around this time, aircraft were being supplied with a bubble sextant. In the past, astronomical observations had depended on a marine sextant, which had limited use because it required a visible horizon. The bubble sextant, so called because it contained a form of spirit level, which by use of mirrors could be seen in a vertical plane, dispensed with the need for a horizon and hence could be used at night, the bubble being illuminated by a small light bulb.

Although many years later, in civil aviation, one had to use the sextant exclusively on occasions, it was vastly different when flying under operational conditions during the war. I found that the only use to which I was able to put it was in the closing stages of a trip, when perhaps over a layer of cloud, and uncertain of position, it was possible to take a sight of the Pole Star, and the reading very quickly converted to give the aircraft's Latitude, a most important piece of information.

The techniques were improved, so much that a Wing Commander Alabaster, I think was his name, actually bombed through cloud using sextant sights, though I heard no report of the accuracy of his effort.

On the nights of August 25th and 27th, under my new skipper's leadership, we took a standard bomb load to Mannheim on both occasions. On each raid, having satisfied the boss as to target identification, we made two successful attacks, summed up by records as: "Flight Lieutenant Casement's crew identified the aiming point and bombed it". What a short simple statement for yet another night of 'anal twitching'!

Finally the night, arrived – August 29th was to be my final visit to the Fatherland – and not a soft target to see me out, either, for the target was Frankfurt, delivering four 500lb bombs and two large canisters of incendiaries.

I would have preferred it if no one had referred to the occasion, but colleagues, and particularly the ground crew, bombarded me with reminders, all well meant, but each one adding to the tension I felt within. Although I told myself "There is no way that they are going to get me tonight," I knew only too well that several chaps had indeed 'got the chop' on just such occasions.

All credit to our pilot who, gentleman that he was, took the positive line and said, "Tomorrow you'll get your well-earned rest, so let's do a good job tonight."

I suppose it had to be, but the activity over the target area was as bad as I had ever seen, yet there was no way that the skipper would go in until I was certain of the aiming point. To make matters worse, there were two main areas of opposition, instead of the planned one. I had no doubt that I had identified the confluence of the Rhine and Main rivers, hence that Frankfurt was dead ahead, but down below all hell was being let loose. Then the penny dropped. This activity was centred over Weisbaden, so either this had been designated a target for other Groups, or some of our people were bombing the wrong target. Anyway, our problem had been solved and we made a determined run at our target and successfully bombed it. We learned later that this was the first occasion on which one hundred aircraft had been sent to Frankfurt, and with no controlled bomber streams in those days, this may well have been the reason for the 'mix up'. Our photograph confirmed our result but the raid record refers to general bombing 'in the Frankfurt area', which rather confirms our view of what was going on.

The long ride home seemed to go on forever, but the feeling of elation when we finally touched down at Woolfox was truly indescribable. At long last, it was over for a while and Casement was the first to offer his hand in congratulation. Did I say a little prayer of thanks? Indeed I did, and more besides. Wouldn't you?

In telling the foregoing part of my story, I hope that I have conveyed an appreciation of two factors. One is the poor state of operational preparedness in Bomber Command, which was countered by the second, the determined efforts of the air and ground crews which, in spite of all, carried us forward to final victory.

There is no doubt that in the run up to the war, politicians and senior officers had forged ahead in the application of misguided policies, often ignoring sensible challenges, and history shows the price which was paid. I believe that, at the end of the day, it was the work of a small number of senior officers down the line, who possessed the great foresight and sound judgement in application who not only managed to convince their leaders of the error of their ways, but inspired the air crews who operated under their leadership and who already had grave misgivings about the conduct of the war, to press home the attack with the necessary vigour and determination. When I think back, I can only conclude that t'was ever thus.

At the conclusion of my tour of operations, I left with one small feeling of sadness in that my name had not been included with those of some of my colleagues for the award of a Distinguished Flying Medal, as a mark of recognition for my efforts. Later on in the war, such awards were almost automatic on completion of a 'tour' if not received for bravery prior to then, but of course they were justly merited when one considers the survival rate and the intensity of opposition later on.

I often ponder on what, if anything, I had done wrong to justify my treatment, but can find no answer. Maybe it was just the luck of the draw.

As it was, I came away with something far more precious which was not granted to many of my friends, namely my life. There, without question, the matter rests.

My operational flying did not cease when I left Bomber Command, which justifies and enables me to continue my story through to the end of hostilities.

FOOTNOTE

During the period in which I served in Bomber Command, indeed from the outbreak of war, other groups, mainly Blenheim and Battle squadrons who were sent to France before the evacuation, were called upon to carry out dangerous, one might even say impossible tasks. They suffered appalling losses which even to this day are not fully appreciated by the British public. Even during the Dunkirk evacuation, when the RAF were harshly criticised by our own Army for their apparent lack of support, they were, in fact suffering tremendous losses whilst trying to hold back the German advance by bombing their support centres.

Sir Winston Churchill did give credit (and I hasten to say, justifiably) to Fighter Command, but hardly a word was said about the Bomber force. It was left to others to sum up the contribution of the RAF and its crews.

John Terraine in his book *The Right of the Line* refers back to historic battles and the fact that the position of honour and greatest danger was to command the vanguard to the right of the line. Applying this to the RAF's wartime effort, J.M. Spaight (Air Historical Branch Monograph) says:

> "It was entitled to hold, and did hold the right of the line in the great struggle for human freedom."

Finally, in tribute to the aircrew under his command, Sir Arthur Harris said:

> "There are no words with which I can do justice to the air crew who fought under my command. There is no parallel in warfare to such courage and determination in the face of danger over so prolonged a period. It was, moreover, a clear and highly conscious courage by which the risk was taken with calm forethought.
>
> It was furthermore the courage of the small hours, of men virtually alone, for at his battle station; the airman is virtually alone.
>
> It was the courage of men with long drawn out apprehension of daily going over the top. Such devotion must never be forgotten."

Wonderful words of appreciation, but sadly, the modern generation seem to be totally unaware of the efforts, courage and sacrifices made. I suppose they can hardly forget what they never knew or have never been told.

CHAPTER THIRTEEN

A Change of Scene at Last

Obviously some heed had been taken of our wishes, should we ever complete a tour, even if such thoughts had been shelved by us whilst busily engaged in other matters. As soon as my records had been checked and my total contribution confirmed, in my case thirty two operations, my posting was announced. I was to attend a Staff Navigation Course at RAF Cranage in Cheshire, following which I would move on to teach navigation and allied subjects to 'new boys'.

What I did not know, for how could I, was that this was to be the first of a number of steps which were to establish my career for many years to come, after I had left the RAF, although much transpired in the Service before that ever came about.

I journeyed to Cranage in the September of 1941, having once again had the pleasure of passing through the mighty Crewe junction on the way. Reporting in, I joined a mixed bag of aircrew, all destined to become teachers of a sort, but many having different reasons for being there in the first instance. Conversation revealed that many were ex-Bomber Command, like myself, and most had completed a tour. One or two chaps seemed a trifle shy and diffident, basically because, as we later discovered, they had little to offer in the general 'line shooting' chat, since they had been selected shortly after completing their basic training as being ideal material to become instructors. Obviously, and sensibly, ability had been put before operational experience in their case.

Practically everyone had navigational experience although there were two marked exceptions. Both were commissioned ranks, and seeing the top button of their uniform jackets undone, one needed no further information as to their service background. This challenging state of undress was the symbolic attire of a Fighter Command pilot. They had both done their share of operations and had been reluctantly forced to rest. Why they were sent to Cranage seemed a mystery and they made it very clear at the outset that they did not wish to teach anybody any subject, particularly navigation, which in any event had never formed a significant part of their work. All they wanted was to return to their units and continue shooting down the Hun.

From day one of our training, it was obvious that, reluctance apart, the navigation theory was not sinking in, and one had to sympathise with them in their efforts to learn.

In due course, one of them, shortly followed by the other, was released from the course and, although the staff instructors still suspected that their apparent inability to learn was staged, I felt that the eventual outcome was best for these two fighter boys and for the RAF.

The course was carefully arranged so that basic theory was revised, supplemented by up to date techniques, and as soon as sufficient information had been absorbed, we were required to leap into the air and put this knowledge into practice.

For this purpose we flew in the faithful old Avro Anson, most of the airborne exercises taking place over The Irish Sea and off to the north west. What was new to me was the opportunity to practice pure navigation with a reasonable number of aids available and without someone trying to blast us out of the sky.

In the classroom, I derived great interest from listening to explanations of the newer instruments; many gyro operated, and thought what a great asset they would have been to us back on the squadron. Unfortunately that was never to be, until larger, better-equipped, aircraft found their way on to the front line.

Starting in a small way, we were called out at intervals to give a short explanation of whatever had been a recent subject of tuition, and quizzed first by the tutor, after which questioning was thrown open to the class.

Eventually, we were given notice of a subject in advance and then required to conduct a full lecture to the rest of the class. They, in turn, were encouraged to be general nuisances and ask relevant, sometimes deliberately stupid, questions.

So one could spend a complete evening learning the subject, only to be floored within minutes, during the lecture, by some totally unexpected question, which may, or may not, have been appropriate, yet you were never quite sure. The result was that it taught us to be thorough in preparation and cautious in response, both being essential in the process of becoming a useful instructor. I confess that I thoroughly enjoyed this stage of my service life and was certainly able to put the knowledge to good use thereafter.

I note from the entry in my log book that a certain Wing Commander Musson stuck his neck out and suggested that I would make a sound instructor... brave man!

At the conclusion of the course, I was granted a weeks leave, during which my posting notice, accompanied by the usual travel warrant, arrived.

Being used to aerodromes in south and central England, the name Wigtown meant very little to me, but the instruction to travel north to Carlisle and then join a Stranraer train to disembark at Newton Stewart said it all. It might just as well have been an overseas posting when I considered the distance from home, but there was one great compensation, which I will detail later, in that this was where I met my wife to be.

I won't dwell on the journey north, other than to say that it seemed endless, that it took place at night in dimly lit, cold, carriages and that after passing Preston it started to rain, and in fact seemed to do so thereafter for most of my time at Wigtown. Even after arrival at Newton Stewart the agony went on, for I had yet to be transported by road to the aerodrome, which was a few miles further south.

Wigtown was one of the few training schools, in this case an AONS (Air Observers Navigation School), operated primarily by civil companies. In Scotland, most of this type of work was carried out by AST (Air Service Training) and I arrived at an interim stage when that company was moving it's staff back to their home base at Perth, while the RAF put their people in to eventually take over the whole unit. For a while this led to a mix of civil and service staff pilots but it worked quite well anyway. The aeroplanes which were used for training were, surprise, surprise, the Avro Anson, and a thoroughly unreliable beast, whose poor performance had left it relegated to such units as ours, the Blackburn Botha. The wreckage of several of the latter could be found on local hills, usually following an engine failure and it's subsequent inability to fly on the remaining one. Any worthwhile book, describing wartime aircraft, will have appropriate opinion of this machine, and I would find it difficult to describe it without resorting to sarcasm at least.

The area in which we now found ourselves, the Mull of Galloway, provided wonderful scenery, when it was not raining, and we did in fact find time to explore our surroundings, initially because there was not much else to do in any spare time which came our way anyway.

First however, I must confess that it was here that I met the young WAAF – much sought after by others I was told – who eventually became my wife and thankfully still is, after 56 years. She had responsibility for catering, in the first instance in the airman's mess, but later in the sergeant's mess.

I was often asked if it was her looks which first caught my eye, but since she used to ride a bicycle to and fro, I'm convinced that it was her shapely knees, frequently, but innocently disclosed, as she rode about, which hooked me. Anyway, like all red-blooded youths, I pursued her with great vigour, and won, which success led to so many happy days in and around the Wigtown area.

Once settled in, a group of us managed to convince the CO that cycling was one of the best forms of recreation and the end product was that we were all issued with service bicycles, enabling us to visit many places off the few bus routes which existed. At a small pub in the village of Whauphill, we won over the heart of the publican's good lady, which led to superb evening meals in the back parlour, and more importantly for me, in an area where ladies were not expected to visit such establishments, my new found lady WAAF was also made welcome.

There were other houses of refreshment which groups of us visited from time to time, such as the Crown at Newton Stewart, which stands on the same site to this day, where our activities were hardly suitable for members of the fairer sex, even understanding young WAAFs, but more of that later.

Apart from a few 'rested' pilots, most of our staff pilots were from overseas, Canada, Australia and New Zealand. They had been held back simply to fly training exercises and did not like this one little bit.

Now I met many such chaps during the war and they don't come any more friendly and competent than our one time Colonial friends, but give them a job which they see as pointless and stand back, because they know just how to register their disapproval.

As they made very clear, they had not come half way round the world simply to conduct training exercises, they wanted to get into the thick of things, to fight and win the war and then return home. The safety of a training job just didn't interest them and difficult though it was for us who had already seen action, to convince them, I think that we could see their point. So this problem produced many disgruntled pilots until, eventually, authority came up with cast iron assurances and so they saw their time out and moved off to squadrons sadly, for many of them, to die all too soon.

I shared a room with one such character from Sydney, Australia, who bent my ear, night after night, maligning the "Pommie bastards who couldn't run a piss up in a brewery" until he too met a pretty young WAAF, when not surprisingly his attitude changed quite suddenly. Unlike my crush on my young lady, his romance didn't last long, but because such affairs were stimulating for his ego, if for nothing else, he then fell in and out of love with many of our other young ladies, almost with the changing phases of the moon.

I know that little changed for him with the passage of time, when after a gap of nearly thirty years, I met up with him again. He had drifted round the world flying for minor aviation companies, but could not return to Oz, because, in his own words, he had "a fortune outstanding in overdue alimony payments" which he could not meet.

Our function in the ground school was to supplement the basic teaching and to bring future navigators up to a point where they could be passed on to OTUs, where the final polish would be added. As each item was taught in classrooms, it was then put into practice in a very primitive form of simulator, which I will explain later and there then followed an air exercise to consolidate. Most of our flying was up to the northwest and over the many islands, where the weather was usually far from perfect.

Although the early sorties proved difficult, since they were just as much of an introduction for myself as for the pupils, I very quickly got to know the routes and landmarks, together with the form that each exercise was to take, and thereafter the flying, when the weather was reasonable, became a pleasure. Although astronomical navigation formed part of the syllabus, very little night flying was accomplished and most of the sextant work was completed by day, using the sun and moon.

I mentioned a simulator earlier on, for want of another name. This consisted of a large room divided into cubicles, wherein, once the pupils were seated, they were taken through a "dry swim", a navigation exercise where all the information was passed verbally from a master plot and they were then required to interpret and act on the information supplied. Not a particularly successful venture since most of the pupils came up with different solutions to the various problems and each had to be sorted out and corrected, leading to much tension and headaches at the end of the day. To add to the difficulties, an old 78rpm record of engine noise was played during the exercises, to add realism, which was the last thing that it did, since it was a harsh penetrating sound guaranteed to mar concentration.

I will not forget this machine since it led to my first taste of parade ground discipline. I found myself in control of one of the exercises, and during a quiet period in the work, the steady monotonous drone of the record must have lulled me into sleep, doubtless aided by a late turn in, on the previous evening.

Feeling a tap on my shoulder, I opened my eyes and glanced up to see the Chief Navigation Instructor standing behind me, but more importantly, another figure stood behind him, displaying a broad pale blue stripe on his sleeve plus other narrower ones. I shot to my feet and apologised, making some lame excuse about night flying effects, and all of this to no less a personage than the AOC (Air Officer Commanding). Little was said and the party moved on, this, as I found out later, being a spot check visit, although I bet that someone there had advanced warning, though obviously not me.

Two days later my name appeared on DROs (Daily Routine Orders) to attend what was then known as the Brighton "B" course. This was a disciplinary course for sinners and was generally regarded as a punishment course. It had been used to lick pilots, guilty of low flying offences, into shape, but as authority soon found out, it was totally inappropriate for them. For my part, I protested to the CO that I could see no reason why I had been singled out for punishment following such a mild offence in the simulator. He, with an angelic smile, said "Not a bit of it Woods! We were asked to send someone, so we decided to send you." I suspected that if I had thanked him for his generosity, it would not have helped me in the future.

The three-week course at Brighton, consisted of muscle breaking PT sessions, unarmed combat, and endless parades and marches through the streets of the town, which was pretty bleak during wartime. The 'criminals' consisted of Officers and NCOs, but we were never separated during parades other than by marching in different flights (groups).

It was a thankless task for the drill NCOs who controlled our marching, since the Officer groups who always led the parade, refused to acknowledge the required pace and, slowing up, caused the following NCO groups to pile into them. All very lacking in discipline, but like most things in the RAF, aircrew managed to create amusement when the going got tough.

One thing was for sure, when we left Brighton; every participant was 100 per cent fit. To show that there was no ill feeling, I asked the CO, on my return, if I could make use of his generous additional training, by lecturing on the duties of an Officer and an NCO which, surprisingly enough, he agreed to. However, at the end of the day, there is usually a price to be paid for being too smart, and so it was for me.

Several of my colleagues had applied for and received commissions and so I decided to put my name forward. I should have known better, for the CO simply said that he had put forward sufficient names for the present.

I still had the good fortune to wear officer-style uniform, since I had been promoted to Flight Sergeant, and shortly after to Warrant Officer First Class.

On the social side, I had fallen hook line and sinker for my lady friend and there were already tentative plans for a wedding. Poor soul, how she suffered, for in spite of our feelings for each other I still joined 'the lads' for frequent pub outings, only to find her patiently waiting at the guard room on my return to see me safely back on the premises.

I have earlier mentioned The Crown at Newton Stewart, a favoured watering hole for pupils and staff alike, and most farewell parties were held on those premises by kind permission of the landlord, one G. Wishart Haggart. Wishart was a lovely old character, with, quite naturally, a liking for the Malt. Added to this, he had an extremely husky voice, and so by late evening, the combination of the two meant that only a long-term customer could understand the words he was uttering.

He nearly caused me a serious injury on one occasion. A group of us were playing darts, when Wishart, without warning, decided to open a floor hatch and descend into the cellar. This he did, but unfortunately as I stepped back, having retrieved my darts from the board, I discovered far too late that he had left the hatch open and down I went, straight on top of our malt laden publican. I suppose the outcome could well have been serious but, in the event, we finished up in a heap, and shared in the hysterical laughter already pouring down on us from the assembled throng up on top. Dear old Wishart, they didn't come any better, but sadly he is now long gone.

In our countryside rides, we organised a new form of entertainment. Having just been issued with service revolvers, we decided to use them for a purpose other than that intended. Pheasant were to be found in our locality, so shoots were organised. I don't recall any success whatsoever, for how could one hit game with a piece of weaponry which could well put a fair sized hole into a brick wall. Never mind, it was another amusing diversion.

My fair lady and I made friends with some of the local folk, one of whom took us ferreting, thus providing something extra for the mess menu. I had heard of the supposed virility of the people in that part of the world, but another of our local friends, already over eighty years of age, took to himself a bride, said to be in her teens, and within weeks was boasting that he was about to become a father. Now I cannot vouch for the truth of this story, although it came to me first hand, but if it was true then it said a lot for the local food and spirits.

To the east of Wigtown was a range of hills, and on one occasion a group of us decided to climb Cairnsmore of Fleet which topped two thousand feet, and we made the journey out and back in the day, finding little of interest on top other than the wrecks of a couple of Bothas.

Slowly but surely, groups of aircrew were beginning to move on. The staff pilots, having served their stint were posted to OTUs prior to moving on to squadrons, but more interestingly to me, those who were deemed to have had a reasonable spell of rest from operations were now being moved back into the fray once more. It seemed that most of the navigators were returning to Bomber Command, mainly to join the recently formed, or re-equipped, Avro Lancaster squadrons.

It was pretty obvious that my turn would come soon, and so inevitably, my lady friend and I decided to formalise our relationship and announce our engagement.

Everything was done to convention, parental approval sought, and then the purchase of the best ring, which I could afford, not that there was much choice in those days. The knot was sealed, and I often wonder if word got out and then led to what so swiftly followed, for in a matter of weeks my posting instructions came through. As I have already mentioned, Bomber Command was almost a certainty, yet all I could discover was that I was to be posted to Lyneham in Wiltshire. The Orderly Room staff had never heard of this station, and neither had I, but what made matters worse was the fact that no specific unit had been quoted.

The CO suggested that it must be one of the recently created 'cloak and dagger' units, which immediately conjured up thoughts of night drops into enemy territory, picking up agents and goodness knows what else.

Little did I know that what was to follow would eventually set the pattern of my life until I finally retired, but right then, I remained a very worried man, more particularly because all of this was happening at a time when the war was really hotting up and we were beginning to get the upper hand, with intense pressure on, and heavy losses in, Bomber Command.

I departed from Wigtown early in May 1943, to the accompaniment of much sobbing and tears, partly offset by assurances from me, of an early marriage. Even then there was a last minute hiccup which could have spelled disaster. Recent short leave periods had been spent with my grandmother who resided at Redhill and next door to whom lived a rather nice young blonde. Not unreasonably I struck up a friendship with her and, like Gwen of days long gone, she presented me with a portrait photograph, which I could carry around if I so chose, and in fact, to my cost, I did. As I stood with my beloved at the camp exit, awaiting transport to the station, the clip on a small attaché case, which I was carrying, snapped and the contents spilled out. Helping me to pick up the bits and pieces what should my lady discover but that photograph. It would not have been so bad had I been revealed as a traitor but, in truth, I was not, though it took a lot of hard talking in a very short time to convince my bride to be that all was well.

Hard though it was, I had to be on my way and so I sat in misery and uncertainty while the train dragged south to London, followed by the tube journey across the big city to join yet another train which would take me to Swindon.

Reflecting on the Redhill visits I find it hard to convince my family of just how harsh the expected standards of behaviour were in those days. As an example, when I first took my intended along to meet my grandmother, that dear soul gave me a thorough dressing down for allowing my girlfriend to hold my arm in public whilst in uniform. It would be fair to say that standards have changed somewhat now, would it not?

Anyway, on to my new home, which was to be at RAF Lyneham. This was a well-established aerodrome, which still exists, sited to the south of the M4, on a form of plateau just a short distance from the town of Calne. Stepping off the train at Swindon, I noticed quite a few RAF personnel of varying ranks and categories, all looking for guidance and all, as I soon discovered, heading for Lyneham. Several trucks stood outside and under the directions of a couple of drivers, we all piled on. Quite obviously, many of my companions had travelled long distances and looked as tired as I felt, but this was not a time for sleeping.

Conversation centred on the possible function of the unit to which we had been posted, but the only sure fact was that we were here to join many others in the process of stepping up operations, in what and to where, was still unknown.

Following the usual booking in procedure, I was allotted a room and retired immediately to bed with orders to report to the adjutant's office in the morning.

Sleep was no problem and I woke much refreshed, breakfasted in a well appointed Sergeants mess, which was chock full of air crew, many wearing decorations for bravery, but still no clue as to what was going on, and I had no inclination to question these chaps as yet.

So on to the Adjutant's office where a duty Corporal took my name and then ushered me in. It was all so relaxed and friendly.

"Come on in old sport and let's tell you what it's all about," was the greeting from an elderly Flight Lieutenant wearing a mix of WW1 and current medal ribbons. Sitting to one side and looking very relaxed was a much younger Squadron Leader, sporting the ribbons of the DSO and DFC, which suggested that he had been rather busy in recent times.

The 'Adj' said that others would be along soon but for the present he'd give me a run down on what was going on. It seemed that this unit had been given a number but was about to be formed into a full squadron, and was then to become No 511 Squadron, hence all the new arrivals.

The aircraft currently being flown were the Armstrong Whit-worth Albermarle, originally intended as a torpedo dropping machine, but now converted to a form of transport, and eventually changed once more towards the end of the war, into a glider towing aeroplane. This, the man said, was used on medium range flights from Lyneham, replaced for long range work by several American Liberator type aeroplanes. So that cleared up the aircraft situation, but as to when and where they were used, that was yet to be revealed. The senior officer, as I then discovered, was 'Dougie' Pascall, a Bomber Command veteran and one of the new flight commanders. It must have been my lucky day for, having gone through my service history, Doug asked the 'Adj' if he could bag me for his crew.

With no knowledge of him or who else was to make up the crew, or of which aircraft we were to fly, I still had a gut feeling that this was the right step and time proved that it was to be so.

CHAPTER FOURTEEN

To Far Away Places with Strange Sounding Names

The following day saw a large group of new boys assembled in the crew room for a general briefing on our future functions. We learned that our job, as a squadron, would be to transport person's unknown and 'certain articles of freight' to a number of points as far east as Cairo, at least for the time being. The Liberator crews would operate from Lyneham to Gibraltar thence direct to Cairo. The Albemarle being a shorter-range aeroplane would operate to North Africa and return via Gibraltar. There was, however, a minor snag in that fuel limitations meant that the latter aircraft would have to land at Portreath in Cornwall on the way out in order to leave our shores with maximum fuel on board. This led to a further problem because quite frequently we landed at Portreath, only to find that, with a south westerly wind, the mist and cloud rolled in from the sea and made take off impossible. Anyone who has spent a holiday in Cornwall will recognise the circumstances I'm sure. An additional snag was the fact that the aerodrome sat virtually on a cliff top on the north coast of Cornwall and with a prevailing wind from off the sea, turbulence at a critical period of take off gave us many a scare and led to a quite few accidents.

A combination of these problems meant that more often than not we arrived at Portreath, only to sit around for a couple of days waiting for the right conditions to allow a safe departure. The nearest towns were Cambourne and Redruth, and in wartime, on a wet and windy night, one was better off by staying on camp and

becoming involved in playing various card games, which we did quite frequently, and as a result of which I learned, from some of our Canadian friends, the art of playing poker, although the lessons did not come cheaply.

I should mention that Dougie now had a full crew, consisting of a co-pilot and a wireless operator/air gunner, plus myself. There were no guns on the aeroplane, so it was his radio skills, which required the third man to be on board.

All flights were classed as operations still, because although we were not carrying bombs, we were flying unarmed aircraft across areas patrolled by the enemy.

The Albemarle, from a navigator's point of view, was a wonderful aeroplane. I sat in solitary splendour up front, rather as in the Mark 4 Blenheim, with a fair sized chart table, surrounded by an expanse of perspex which allowed perfect all round vision. Above the navigators head was a perspex "astrodome" to allow sextant work, but there was a luxurious innovation which made one feel important, for by operating a cable control, the navigators seat could be slowly raised up towards the dome, so that one could sit in comfort whilst at war with the heavens.

Our route south, bearing in mind that Europe was still occupied, as was most of North Africa, took us from a point well to the south west of the Scilly Isles, thence almost due south across Biscay, continuing on, until it was safe to head for the African coast.

There were few aids, other than the sextant, and cloud frequently precluded use of that facility. However, mainly for use when homeward bound, a radio 'fixer' service had been established, whereby, as soon as it was safe to break radio silence, the wireless operator contacted a master station, situated at Butser, on a hill in the west country. This call alerted two other radio stations and all three then took radio bearings on our transmission, which enabled them to plot our position and pass details back to us. These "fixes" were not always accurate and so

Opposite page: The Avro York.

had to be classified as Class 1, 2 and 3, but even category 3, the lowest, was better than nothing if one had had a troublesome flight north.

I well recall my first trip in some detail. As I mentioned earlier in this record, I have been asked how I can remember such detail, and if a lot of it isn't just imagination and dressing. Hard though it may be to understand, my enthusiasm for flying coupled with the endless changes in scene and circumstance, make recollection easy, in the main.

We had been briefed for a flight to Ras El Ma, returning via Gibraltar, and in due course dropped in to Portreath in order to 'fill up'. The weather meant that we had every chance of getting away on time, and with a veteran like Dougie in command, we had no fears of the take off over the cliff. Incidentally, some pilots regarded Portreath as a jinx field, but in fact, most of the accidents, which took place, were due to pilot error, perhaps partly due to apprehension.

The weather forecast was for broken medium level cloud most of the way, becoming part cloud cover and then clear over Morocco.

Joining our aeroplane we awaited the arrival of our passengers, who were spirited out in blacked out cars, so that we rarely saw, or for that matter cared, who they were. VIPs they may have been, but the rear end of our aeroplane was hardly built for comfort.

No problem with take off and we headed up through cloud, with occasional glimpses of a bright full moon above.

Dougie decided that as we were below the freezing level, we would play safe and level off in cloud until well south, just in case we bumped into a German patrol, who were operating out of French coastal aerodromes at that time, and out over the close Atlantic.

So for a couple of hours we chugged along, with no navigational facilities, until Dougie decided that we could pop our nose out on top.

In spite of this start to the flight, I felt reasonably relaxed because for a while, unlike many of our less fortunate chums, we were heading away from shot and shell.

Having operated the engine superchargers, our skipper raised the nose and up we headed. A little turbulence as we ascended, with an increase in the brightness as we neared the cloud tops. Then, in a flash, the scene changed dramatically, first with intermittent flashes of bright light and then, almost as if under the action of a switch, we burst out on top. The moon, a magnificent white ball up aloft and the cloud-bank, now fast receding below like a vast silver blanket. A truly awe inspiring sight whether in wartime or peace, a sight not given to many to see and appreciate.

Climbing well clear, the aircraft was levelled off and I set about the business of establishing just where we were. I confess that my first attempt at an astro fix was not too brilliant and was best summed up as indicating that we were somewhere west of Bordeaux.

The cloud began to break below, and I held off from further sextant work since well ahead and off to the east was a faint yellow glow below the cloud. I had been advised, but it had slipped my mind, that Portugal and Spain, being neutral, had no reason to black out and what I could see was the lights of one of the coastal towns. Even this, useful though it was, was not needed, for flashing ahead, quite clearly, was the coastal light at Cape Finnistere. We had been given the characteristics of all such marine lights, and how useful that information proved to be.

So, with an eye to the east for the next few hours, we cruised along checking our position with a reasonable degree of accuracy until we passed off Cape St Vincent and the coast swung off to the east and disappeared out of sight. At this point it was safe to break radio silence and contact Gibraltar, who came back with an assurance that the weather at our destination was clear. We did, of course, use morse code for communications but were not unduly concerned about security for two reasons. One was that Lisbon and Algeciras were espionage centres and reports of all RAF movements were almost certainly passed on, but the other was the skill of our radio men. The speed at which they operated the morse key, and this was a matter of pride, must have made our signals difficult to read with accuracy. I do say this with tongue in cheek, of course.

We altered our heading on to a southeasterly direction, by which time the first signs of greying sky in the east heralded the arrival of morning twilight.

Cloud was beginning to break up and as the sea became visible, I noticed that it was far from calm. Contact had now been made with our destination, and for my part I had tuned in a radio beacon set up by the Americans at Port Lyautey, and was delighted to see that it lay almost dead ahead, just where I had hoped it would appear. The sky took on a dark blue hue, then pink, yellow, and finally, as that great red ball popped up over the horizon and we were flying in daylight.

As we commenced a shallow descent, with the object of gaining more speed, I fixed my gaze ahead, eager for my first sight of Africa. The sea below, which I had assumed would be blue, was, to my surprise, a dirty grey and extremely choppy, so there was quite a wind blowing down there.

Distracted for a moment, I was quickly alerted when Dougie yelled, "There it is! Coast ahead!" Of course there was no great credit in this landfall in a navigational sense, for sooner or later we had to hit Africa, but what was important was to hit it in the right place. I now saw the long stretch of sandy coastline, but with no prominent feature to assist until, combining the radio beacon reading and a large identifiable river estuary to the north, I was able to confirm that we were pretty well on our required track.

So over the coast, and here we were, Africa, or Morocco to be more precise, and no one waiting to shoot us down. We tuned our radio in to a very low powered beacon close by our destination and it was now left to Dougie to home in on it, while I sat back and took in the sights, such as they were. Sand dunes, turning to scrub, with patches of greenery here and there and an increasing number of tracks, which became tarmac covered as we moved on, and small whitewashed huts or houses nearby on either side. I heard the skipper contact our destination on the short-range radio telephony channel and obtain clearance to land. I never had a chance to view Ras El Ma from the air at this time because we made a straight in approach and landing and my first sight was of tarmac below and a few buildings off to one side. We taxied in, and while I was busy stowing my gear, a couple of camouflaged staff cars pulled alongside and away went whoever it was that we had just delivered.

The airfield was not far from Fez, the old capital, and once we had carried out the necessary arrival procedures, we were taken to a small but very comfortable hotel for the night. Here we settled back to enjoy new pleasures, such as wine with our food, fresh exotic fruit and an overnight laundry service. In fact we could not avail ourselves of the latter as we had to be up at the crack of dawn for the short hop to Gibraltar.

Thoroughly rested we were woken early, transported out to the aerodrome where our aeroplane had been serviced, refuelled and stood ready to go, and we were up, up and away. The weather being clear, we could see Gibraltar before we made the short crossing from North Africa, but now came the important require-ment for the approach. We had already given the control people details of our flight, but more was required. Approaching Europa point, the southern most tip of the rock, we had to fire off the colours of the day as confirmation of identity. With memories of our Naval friends off the Humber estuary in mind, I now did so with a feeling of trepidation. A great sigh of relief when the man down below gave us some sort of green signal and off around the eastern side of the imposing looking rock we went.

In those days, the runway was very short, and with even moderate wind-flow off and around the rock, landings were frequently hairy, the air being extremely turbulent with strong cross wind elements, hence the number of incidents and accidents and the many occasions when aircraft were forced to 'go around again' at the last moment.

Thankfully we were with a veteran pilot who also knew the Rock, so all went well and we were soon taxiing back to our allotted spot, noting with much interest, the activity to the north of the runway where stood the clearly visible town of La Linea.

With shortages at home, shopping was a priority and so our first call was to the town where we topped up with fresh fruit and spirits before returning to the north camp for a pre-flight rest.

Night departures were essential for obvious reasons, but they brought their own problems. I have already mentioned the short runway, but in addition to this, once airborne, when taking off to the west, we had to avoid Spanish neutral airspace. On this occasion, we taxied to the far end of the runway – in fact almost onto the beach – in order to use every foot of available space. Then we turned to face the dim runway lights and the darkness beyond. Doug opened up the throttles, stood on the brakes and then, with a yell, released them allowing us to trundle slowly forwards – too slowly for my liking. As the speed built up I could see very few runway lights remaining, and so, sitting in front, I held on to the sides of my seat and waited. The faint lights of Algeciras could be seen in the distance when with a seemingly gentle tug, the aeroplane came 'unstuck'. I saw the sea rushing beneath but only for a brief moment because almost immediately the aircraft was put into a tight left turn, passing over naval and other vessels moored in and around the harbour as we headed out for the Straits.

Doubtless the watchers across the bay had by now signalled our departure as we headed west, looking for the lighthouse at Tariffa from which point we would head further to the west to put us off Cape St Vincent and then on to our track for home.

The return flight was uneventful, except that headwinds caused us to eat into our fuel, necessitating a landing at St Mawgan, in Cornwall, to top up and then fly on to Lyneham.

It is interesting to note that even in those early days, we had HM Customs based at Lyneham, and also the Service Security team, who eventually became involved in sorting out certain dubious trade activities which, developed, and which they rapidly scotched.

We learned that the squadron, for the present, would be operated almost like a charter airline, remaining on call to go almost anywhere at any time, with crews available on a roster basis.

As things were comparatively quiet, this gave us a break of about three weeks, during which time we got out and about and sorted out, in our opinion, the best local pubs. Dougie had earlier asked me why I had not received commissioned rank and, having given him the best explanation which I could think of, he gave me a broad wink, which effectively said "leave it to me". I had no idea how such matters were handled, what I did know was that in May 1943 I was duly commissioned and appointed to the exalted rank of Pilot Officer. A clothing allowance fast came my way, and off I went to London, where at Burton' clothing store in Tottenham Court Road I was duly kitted out. I do remember my return to Lyneham when, now conscious of the fact that the rank called for a salute, I approached the airman on duty at the gate, and raising my hand, half in anticipation, we were both amused when I saluted him before he had a chance to 'throw one up'.

This stemmed from the fact that in wartime there was little time for such niceties as at Cranwell and the strict officer-training course.

Time passed quickly and in due course we were ordered to operate another Albemarle flight, this time to Tripoli, the capital of Libya.

Events had moved fast in North Africa and our Desert Army from the east with the Americans from the west had pushed Rommel and his Africa Korps up into Tunisia, prior to sending them packing altogether.

On the appointed afternoon, we boarded another group of unknown individuals and headed for Portreath, where after a rapid refuelling we were airborne at twilight and heading once more for Africa. We followed the standard route, this time without the advantage of a moon and arrived at Gibraltar in darkness. Fortunately, with a westerly wind, we were able to approach from the seaward side thus allowing a long steady approach and a smooth landing. With refuelling under way, I noticed that our radio man had scrounged a lift on a service vehicle and was off into town. This seemed somewhat strange since we normally made our purchases on the homeward flight.

All was eventually to be revealed when we reached our next stop, the port and city of Algiers. This sector was so pleasant, because we departed after sun up and headed out over the blue waters of the Mediterranean, to enjoy the type of flying which I had not experienced for many a year. The flight was straightforward in that our American friends, by now operating their MATS (Military Air Transport System), had set up a very powerful radio beacon at Algiers, which indicated our destination direction very clearly. A few hours later and the coast hove into sight, with a large collection of war vessels off shore.

Duly cleared in, we headed for Maison Blanche, the aerodrome, where we were greeted by a small group of our own people, who shepherded our passengers away and then drove us to what appeared to be a large villa.

We were very tired by now and so after a pleasant meal and a few glasses of Algerian plonk, we needed no rocking to sleep that night.

Called at the crack of dawn, we made our way back to the airfield and after preparing our flight plan, our "customers" were boarded and away we went. I did notice that this airfield and a couple of adjacent ones were teeming with American transport aircraft, for when the Americans go in, they do it in style.

Our early departure was standard practice because the land, particularly sand, heats up very quickly and resultant turbulence can be troublesome. Our initial track took us south across the Atlas Mountains, after which as we reached the northern edge of the Sahara, we would head east for Libya.

The mountains being fairly close, we had little time to gain a lot of height, hence we climbed laboriously over steep slopes and valleys, just managing to hold on to our breakfast during the bumpy ride over the top.

In due course we reached our planned height and things settled down a little, while not too far ahead we could make out the thick yellow haze over the desert.

On our run east I looked with interest on the changes from cultivation to scrub and then to endless sand in a variety of colours. Most of the fighting having taken place to the north, there was not a lot of evidence of warfare down below, and it wasn't long before we were chatting on the radio to our man at Castel Benito, the aerodrome south of Tripoli. We spotted the tarmac road leading south and after a wide circuit landed smoothly and taxied in to find our passengers whisked away almost before the engines had shut down.

Having been under German and Italian control, until very recently, things were a little chaotic to say the least, with American aircraft in strength, plus a fair number of South African Air Force planes, and just a couple of RAF machines. Accommodation was based on a first come first served basis, hence the Americans were in town, the South Africans in what remained of the permanent buildings and the Brits, where else but in tents in a vineyard just outside the camp gates.

The aerodrome was littered with the wrecks of German and Italian aircraft and, in spite of the circumstances, it was a collectors paradise. I confess to carrying the control column and firing gear from a Fiat fighter, back to the UK, only to give it away many years later.

Sleep was difficult to achieve and we were only too happy to be on our way next day, for the run home via Gibraltar, which provided nothing of particular interest.

I mentioned our radio man's strange behaviour at Gibraltar, and all was revealed some time later when he tried to involve me. He was purchasing good quality wristwatches at knock down prices and then carrying them through to Algiers where they were sold to our American friends at a vast profit. This racket, for that's what it was, was one of the reasons for the SIB (Special Investigation Branch) being based at Lyneham, and as our routes extended further east, they were kept very busy.

Chatting with Doug one day, I remarked on the number of well-decorated pilots on the squadron, and learned a lot about their presence. Some came from Bomber Command with a wealth of experience in handling large aeroplanes, which would soon be put to good use as newer larger transport aircraft arrived. Others already had experience in long range flying, one example being Charles Hughesden, who had flown the first twin-engined DH Comet in the pre-war England to Australia air race. Another was the charming 'Ossie' Morris, who shortly I after met him was whisked back to the picture industry, his original profession, to continue making films, presumably with propaganda in mind, although, years later, I noticed his name in the credits for a number of popular films, his greatest, for my money, being the leading light in the filming of "Lawrence of Arabia".

So we had a strong team, chock full of veterans, and hardly a new boy in sight, and if one thing was for sure, it was that this squadron soon became regarded as the best, in it's particular field, and stayed so until finally disbanded, long after the war.

Although the RAF and civil airlines had flown through to Asia before the war, it was the build up of transport flying, initially by 511 Squadron, which pioneered the new routes east.

Dotted along these routes were small landing strips, but at a couple of spots, namely Heliopolis (Cairo) and Habbaniyah close to Baghdad, show piece aerodromes had been constructed, indeed the field at "Hab" was almost like a small self contained town with tree lined roads and permanent buildings housing every required facility.

Our team continued, as a happy little unit, to fly out to Gibraltar, Morocco and Libya, and eventually after the Germans had been booted out, up into Tunisia.

However, in mid August 1943, another "Dogsbody" job was suddenly thrown my way. I reported to the flight office as ordered to find that as one of the unit navigators had been struck down by some bug or the other, I was to join a Flight Lieutenant Sanders and his crew, to operate a Liberator flight through to Cairo, via Gibraltar. This being wartime, there was no provision for any sort of equipment briefing, it being assumed that you could navigate any aircraft, regardless. Our departure was scheduled for midnight that night which gave me a chance to wander out and have a brief look at this big American ship, where, oddly enough, my crew position was on a platform to the rear. A spin off I suppose from a conversion to RAF requirements.

I had not flown in a large aeroplane, since the Manchester, so after the Albemarle this seemed a giant, and, as I was soon to find out, a noisy one at that.

We departed on time for what was a routine, but faster than usual, run down to the Rock, where we arrived in time for a light breakfast and then off to bed prior to another night departure.

On this occasion, our take off was to the east, hence once airborne we had a clear run and climb out over the sea, with no obstructions whatsoever. Fortunate really, because this aerodrome was somewhat limiting for large aeroplanes until the runway was extended, and older readers may well recall that the Polish wartime leader, General Sikorski was killed in a Liberator crash there.

Our climb to altitude was through cloud, giving us a spell of thumps and bumps until, emerging out on top, we settled down to a smooth ride on.

Our route was to take us over Algiers, towards Tripoli and then across the desert territory where not so long ago, fierce tank battles had been fought. Navigational facilities were few and far between and so for the first time I was able, indeed had, to settle down to regular sextant work, comprising so called three star fixes. The Liberator was a very stable aircraft in clear air and so I gained a great deal of confidence from my results.

The radio man had contacted Cairo and we learned that our destination was fog bound, but, as so regularly happened, as soon as the Sun got to work, we knew that it would burn off the fog or raise it to low cloud.

We spotted El Alamein, and then picked up the tarmac coast road, which led to Cairo, but unfortunately, just ahead, it disappeared under the fog bank, now clearly visible in the early morning light.

This was another event, which I recall well, because it was fun. The fog began to lift and break into very low cloud through which we could see the road, which eventually passed alongside our destination, a landing ground which, if my memory serves me correctly, was listed as LG224.

As we hurtled along, having already descended to a thousand feet or so, we had frequent glimpses of the desert through the growing number of gaps in the low cloud, and could even see service vehicles heading along the road. Suddenly "Sandy" yelled "Hold tight everyone" as he threw the huge beast into a tight descending turn through a fairly large break in the cloud only to break clear, down below, at a few hundred feet above the sand. Of course, this was not unduly dangerous as there was no high ground in the vicinity and certainly no other aircraft or air traffic control, so having picked up the tarmac road again, we sat on top of it, hurtling along at high speed and undoubtedly scaring the pants off of some of the drivers down below, although they could not see us until we had passed over. With the landing ground ahead, and even after an eleven hour flight, Sandy "greased" the Liberator on to the runway and then off to our dispersal point where we off-loaded our "customers".

The "slip crew" system had just been introduced and so another crew were standing by to take our aeroplane home while we were to await the next one through, four days later. We didn't relish the thought of sleeping in tents for four nights, but at least we had a chance to visit Cairo.

Old hands will recall the "boot black" menace in that city and we arrived before it had been cleared up. These dirty little urchins would pester service personnel to take a shoeshine, and if refused, they flicked some dreadful gunge on to one's footwear, which was difficult to remove. The Army lads did much to punish them, but these little horrors persisted and unless you knew the drill, you were trapped every time.

One delightful compensation was Groppi's, a restaurant and ice cream parlour, close by one of the Nile bridges. I'll wager that there aren't many service lads who didn't visit this spot for a Knickerbocker Glory or the like.

Would you believe that another "not to be missed" spot in Cairo, was the Museum of Hygiene, wherein one could see plaster casts of the end product of untreated VD. Strange, but true, for times were different then.

Our stop over soon passed and off home we flew, having a ten-hour rest at the Rock, on the way.

During the few days of our absence, great changes, once rumoured, were now about to take place. The Albemarle was to be replaced by the Douglas DC3 (Dakota), and in the not too distant future, the Avro York would replace the Liberator. It was evident that we were on the move and now destined to grow fast.

The Dakota, which is still flying as a type today, was a wonderful old ship and the York was an offshoot from the Lancaster, having the same wing and Rolls Royce Merlin engines, but with a huge box like fuselage slung underneath.

Since Dougie was a flight commander, he was one of the first to be converted to the Dakota, hence our crew would benefit from the change almost immediately.

While Doug was undergoing his conversion training I managed to scrounge a ride on a Liberator which was heading for Northern Ireland and the skipper agreed to drop me off at Wigtown, and pick me up on the way back. I found my beloved as soon as I had landed, and without permission, she slid off and we found a secluded room at the rear of the mess, locked the door and had an hour or so for a chat, a kiss and a cuddle, mostly chat I hasten to add, because our planned marriage had become an important subject by then. It was over all too soon but, for both of us, it had been a small morale booster.

After a couple of week's break, we made our first trip in the Dakota, to Ras El Ma, whence we were to fly on to Tunis and then to Malta. It was on this trip that I learned that one can never afford to be too frivolous with conduct in the air since it is for sure that there is a price to be paid.

I have frequently related this story, but it does no harm to repeat it. Having left Morocco, we were bowling along quietly heading eastwards when I noticed that both pilots, having engaged the autopilot, were sitting back, almost literally with their feet on the instrument panel.

This didn't seem fair as the radio man and I were quite busy. A quick consultation, and having emptied the metal containers, which held our air, crew rations, synchronising our actions, we removed the lids only to bring them down simultaneously on to the boxes with an ear shattering crash. What a sight to behold, as both pilots almost shot out of their seats in fright. Roars of laughter from behind soon dampened by the outraged dressing down from Doug, until he saw the funny side.

However, the laugh was to be on us and not thanks to any retaliation from Doug.

An hour or so later, with everything running smoothly, there was suddenly an awful bang and a surge from one of the engines. The radio man looked at me in alarm, and in the normal course of events I too would have been disturbed, but I had no doubt, and indeed said so, that this was the boys up front getting their own back on us, only they weren't. An urgent call from Doug to the radio man asking him to contact Algiers and to prepare them for an emergency landing. This, coupled with the dreadful noise from the engine made the gravity of the situation abundantly clear.

The Dakota was capable of flying on one engine, but with no positive clue as to the precise nature of the problem from the engine instruments, the priority was to get us down on to the ground. It was certainly a worrying period as we slowly descended and altered heading for Algiers, where accompanied by an ambulance, fire tender and crash truck; Doug made a textbook single engined landing. I don't recall the nature of the problem, but being an American base there was no trouble in isolating and correcting the engine fault, thus enabling us to carry on, after a night's rest.

Although there was no connection between our little joke and the engine failure, I vowed never to misbehave in that manner again, and I never did, being ever fearful that there was always punishment to follow. Superstition if you will, but it cured me of bad habits in flight.

We managed just sufficient time to visit Carthage whilst transiting Tunis and then it was on to the beleaguered island of Malta.

The island had taken a terrible hammering and as we made our way from the airfield to the RAF rest house at St Pauls Bay, we passed endless masses of rubble from damaged buildings, very like London at it's worst except that the debris was ochre in colour from the sandstone I suppose, rather than grey/black, back home. Grand Harbour was full of vessels, some of them resting on the sea-bed as evidence of the concentrated bombing.

The rest house was on the north side of the island, alongside St Pauls Bay, and provided reasonably comfortable accommodation and food, but in addition, some enterprising soul had "found" a few canoes, and so, being autumn, we were able to paddle around in the warm sea and truly relax and wind down. Thankfully no enemy aircraft visited during our stay, they were too busy in Italy I guess.

From its reputation, we just had to visit the notorious "Gut" in Valetta and this was quite an experience. I don't know how many bars or houses of ill repute existed down there, but I suspect that there were probably too many to count. Certainly, with the large military presence, every taste was catered for, as we found out on this visit. Our first port of call was, I think, the Bulldog but it soon became apparent that we weren't welcome unless we carried handbags, which suggested that this 'pub' was incorrectly named and should have been called Pink Poodle. We moved on, but at the next bar we not only found the beer terribly expensive, but the attention of the fair young maids, trying their best to remove all of our clothing, forced a rapid retreat. We were totally unprepared for this kind of treatment for it never seemed to have happened in pubs back home!

Anyway, we had made the duty run and thereafter could nod our heads wisely whenever the Gut became a subject for discussion. In 1987 I took my wife on holiday to Malta and made a point of visiting that same street, only to find that it now appeared as just another street full of bars.

My abiding memory is not just of the incidents which I have already mentioned, but of the noise and the American western saloon atmosphere, with bodies hurtling out through doors on to the street, most of them wearing naval uniform, and all seeming to be deliriously happy.

As a crew, we shunted to and fro the Mediterranean, until, quite suddenly, Dougie informed us that he was about to be posted away, and that we would now be reallocated to another "driver".

I suppose that he had fulfilled his task in getting one section of the squadron fully effective and his talents were now needed elsewhere. A great pilot, and many years after the war I bumped into him again, at which time he was in process of setting up a small airline in Northern Ireland, Emerald Airways, so you could never keep a good man down.

While re-crewing was in process, I was once again asked to fill in for a sick navigator, and operate on a Dakota flight to the Azores, via Gibraltar. There were two interesting aspects to this flight, the first being that I had barely heard of the Azores, other than as a staging post for our American friends crossing the Atlantic, but secondly, the flight was to take place over the Christmas period, which was unwelcome but suggested urgency.

Not a very good start because, on arrival at Gibraltar, a strong cross wind prevented landing and we had to fly to the American base at Port Lyautey in Morocco, until things improved at the Rock, which they did in a matter of hours.

While most of the service personnel and Gibraltarians were gearing up to celebrate, we spent a few hours, on Christmas Eve, in snatching what sleep we could, before our departure at 3am on Christmas Day.

There was great relief when we were airborne on time, since everyone below could now get on with the fun. There was nothing very special about the westward flight, because although I busied myself with sextant work over the sea, there was the comfort of two very powerful radio beacons at either end of the sector, and the beacon at Lagens (Azores) indicated "dead ahead", almost from our departure time.

We arrived late on Christmas morning, to be received by a not too happy ground crew, but arrival procedures were completed in record time, and then we strangers were invited to join local staff in getting the delayed celebrations under way. It was fortunate that we were scheduled for a two-day stop over, because our crew imbibed to excess and not one of us had any sensible recollection of precisely what transpired, or where.

However, duty called, and as loyal airmen, we appeared bright eyed and bushy tailed at the appointed time for the flight home.

The weather forecast was far from satisfactory, giving layered, and cumulus type, cloud with freezing level at a few thousand feet, hence a great risk of icing.

I had experienced icing conditions before, but this flight proved to be one for the book.

We departed on time but climbing away went straight into on what was a dark and dirty night. The skipper attempted to find a gap between layers of cloud, but the turbulence indicated that we were already in cumulus cloud. An attempt was made to climb up through but things got worse with heavy rain and hail and still no sign of coming out on top. An early reaction was that we should turn back, but a fresh attempt was made by descending and then trying to fly on, accepting the turbulence on the basis that it couldn't last forever.

The "bumps" did ease a little but the precipitation did not and very soon the engines began to indicate their disapproval by starting to give audible signs of rough running. Looking out on to the wings, we could all see the build up of clear ice on the leading edges, with more on the engine cowlings. The pilot switched on the engine and airframe de-icing equipment, which became partially effective, but most disconcerting, because as ice broke off, some of it struck the metal fuselage with a resounding bang, bringing back memories of shrapnel from days, hopefully well behind us.

All in all, it was most disturbing, and every one of us was keyed up, certainly frightened, and wondering what would happen next.

A decision was made, and it turned out to be the correct one, which was to descend to below freezing level, and then to fly on, taking whatever came our way.

So it was that miles out over the Atlantic, we came down to a couple of thousand feet, and flew on in rain and turbulence, with fingers crossed.

Mind you, even this was a partial relief because, during our descent, the ice broke off in large chunks and I nearly jumped out of my skin each time a lump hit metal.

Very slowly, conditions improved and the temperature rose as we moved north-eastwards, although, even as we approached the Scilly Isles, we were still in and out of cloud. Flying at low level, and with engine problems, we had burned off far too much fuel, so it was into Portreath once more to pick up sufficient fuel to get us home. I suspect that our poor passengers had had enough by then, because they knew little of what was going on, other than the mixture of worrying noises and, after telephone contact with authority, they cheerfully made their way on by road.

So that was another flight which I remember in detail, and just to round it off, it all happened over Christmas. Weren't we just the luckiest of chaps?

Crewing had been sorted out and in mid January 1944, I joined Flight Lieutenant (Bob) Hepburn, as part of his team, to continue flying Dakotas, until a year or so later when the long awaited Avro Yorks began to arrive.

One great asset with the dear old Dakota, was the modern equipment and comfort. All crew seats were comfortably padded, as was the interior of the fuselage on the flight deck. No bare metal or projections to snag one's clothing, and very sophisticated instrument presentation and performance. In short, an aeroplane, which acknowledged that it's crew, had not just been slung on as an afterthought. Oh that some of the RAF machines had been similarly built. Still mustn't complain, in every other respect, we built the best.

With Bob, we shuttled to the various Middle East destinations, but by now our passenger loads were no longer "hidden" and seemed to consist mainly of senior officers, in uniform.

Then a very pleasant surprise It was decided to set up a through service to Ceylon (Sri Lanka), still using the Dakota, but operating the slip crew system whereby a crew would operate a couple of sectors and then hand over to another crew who would take the aeroplane on, whilst the first crew awaited the next plane, which they, in turn, would take on.

We set off on one such flight at the end of April, the first stages of which were more than familiar until we arrived at Cairo, after which it was all new to me.

We had been provided with a form of route manual, but other than for main airfields the detail was very sketchy. Many of the remote sites were shown from ancient photographs accompanied by words such as "thought to hold this or that fuel" or " said to have a hard taxi surface", which information seemed to originate from the early thirties, or even before.

Our route was to take us up to north Lebanon, after which, with a modicum of luck, we would pick up the old oil pipe line which crossed the desert from northern Iraq down to the Haifa region and then "cheat", by following it for a good part of the way.

We first flew across the Gaza strip and then over the Jordan valley, and the bordering hills until looking ahead, I could see the vast yellow brown desert so beloved of Lawrence and Doughty. I noticed that in the early stages, it wasn't as featureless as I had expected, there being a few tracks, almost qualifying as roads, and then, crossing at right angles, the railway line, which had figured so prominently in the earlier war with the Turks. Anyway, my interest was more in navigation, and I was certainly pleased to see ahead, the dark line of the road, which ran alongside the pipeline. These dark lines were in fact compacted sand which had been covered with oil and the sun then baked it into a hard surface, suitable for road transport, and in some areas to form a landing surface for aircraft.

Alongside this particular road there were a number of landing strips spaced at roughly equal distances apart, to provide emergency landing fields, and eventually, very low powered radio beacons were installed at some of them.

Picking up the pipeline, Bob followed it, while I took time off to look to the south into the desert. It wasn't quite featureless, as there were many colour changes, dried up wadis (riverbeds), and numerous dark rock outcrops. I also noted groups of black shapes, widely spaced, which I learned in time, were Bedouin tents. However, I had to get back to the job in hand, for very soon the pipeline and road would track off to the north and we were heading for Habbaniyah. Visibility began to fall, just as forecast, due to rising sand, and so I provided Bob with a compass heading for our last checkpoint before Habbaniyah, the desert fort at Rutbah.

As our estimate for Rutbah approached, we descended into the dusty atmosphere, peering ahead into the murk, for sight of our checkpoint.

Some alarm when it failed to appear and just as we were about to consider our next move, there it was, dead ahead, a large walled fort, looking just like something out of Beau Geste and which could only be Rutbah, but in an instant and in the poor visibility, it had gone. A quick heading adjustment for Bob and we were on the final run in.

Radio contact confirmed that visibility at our destination was just about on acceptable limits, and the powerful radio beacon beckoned us on.

I must confess that it was not an easy approach and landing for Bob at a strange airfield, but being a major aerodrome, it was not easy to lose it during the circuit, and in a few minutes a weary and relieved crew were being transported to comfortable rooms on what resembled a bungalow estate. Incidentally, anyone who followed the recent Gulf conflict will recognise this as one of the main Iraqi aerodromes, provided originally by the RAF and government contractors, who obviously could not have visualised the future use of that field as an essential unit to an enemy.

Habbaniyah was the Air Headquarters for Iraq, and we were told that we had arrived just as the staff were about to hold a formal dining in night, to which we would all be welcome.

Like so much of what happened during my service life, I well remember an extremely amusing incident which occurred that night involving one of air crew's harshest critics," the penguin", in this case, I believe, a long serving ground based administrator.

I had no hard feelings against such people in general, but there were a few who had lived a cosy existence in the peace time service and resented the arrival of these young air crew upstarts, who often gained rapid promotion for no reason which they could understand, poor chaps.

Anyway, after the formal dinner and toasts, the tables were cleared of crockery and cutlery and we settled down to an evening of songs and yarns, led by the AOC on the top table. These sessions, at home, usually degenerated into a "sing a song, tell a tale or show your arse" event, and this one seemed to be heading that way.

Seated at the end of our sprig was the aforementioned penguin, who had been talking in an unnecessarily loud voice to impress, which, in fact, it did not.

When he was sure that he had maximum attention, he ordered us to hold our glasses and for stewards to clear the table completely. He then virtually commanded two of his fellow officers to position themselves at the far end of the table, while he prepared himself for whatever it was that he was going to offer as entertainment. Removing his jacket, he made a short take off run, let out a blood curdling scream and then launched himself face down on to the highly polished surface of the table, arms spread out like wings. Under the initial thrust he sailed gracefully towards the end of the table, only to disappear off the far end into a crumpled heap on the floor, all to the accompaniment of cheers from the assembled throng, including his two chums standing watch at the end. The fool, in his arrogance, had forgotten to warn them that they were supposed to stop his "flight" at the table end, but who were they to assume that that's why they were there... I wonder.

He finally rose, much battered but not in a position to admonish his chums in the face of thunderous applause. Of course we all knew that we were just playfully feeding the fools ego, and I'm sure that he must have been conscious of the fact that he was being mocked, but to give him credit, he took it like a trouper, although I bet that the event proved an object lesson too.

It was certainly a most enjoyable evening and we all slept soundly that night. 24 hours later, and off once again over new territory, this time down the Gulf to Bahrein.

Initially we followed the Euphrates down to the confluence with the Tigris, just south of Basra, thence out over the sea with the small fishing village of Kuwait off to the right. The only sign of things to come was a long jetty constructed to take the first of the tankers calling to pick up oil, now beginning to emerge to the south. I think that there was a small landing strip there, and a few buildings. Looking at Kuwait City today one can well judge the power of oil.

No problems with navigation, as our track crossed and re-crossed the yellow barren coast, the only sign of life being a development at the headland of Ras Tanura, which a year or so later became a vast complex of oil storage tanks, so rapidly did oil exploration advance.

A signal from Bahrein warned us of poor visibility with rising sand. It seems strange, bearing in mind that Bahrein sits at the head of the Island of Manama, but in fact the dust was drifting across from the Arabian mainland.

The aerodrome was at Muhurraq, on a small island connected to the main island by a causeway, and the runway surface consisted of some sort of crust of compacted salt and sand.

On the approach, with cockpit windows open, we had a sample of what was to follow as salt laden air, with a percentage humidity factor of nearly 100%, flowed in at a temperature of around 35 degrees Centigrade. Visibility was down, but acceptable, and we were soon down and taxying in to the refuelling point. Perspiration poured off us, and we almost envied the ground crews wearing nothing but sandals and shorts.

No air conditioning for anyone, and we were transported to shacks which consisted of what seemed to be palm frond sides with huge gaps at the top and bottom, to allow the steam, which passed as air, to flow through. I believe that these "dwellings" were called Barastis.

Yes, it was that bad, and how we truly pitied the poor souls who were required to serve there, although their term was measured in months in those early development years, and rightly so.

The locals seemed to survive on fishing and, we were told, pearl diving.

There was no shortage of alcohol and our American friends with the mainland oil companies used to come over and endeavour to drink the island dry, Arabia having long since prohibited alcohol.

It is true that, in normal circumstances, RAF aircrew had the edge on others when it came to sleeping accommodation, but at Bahrein, forget it.

Our quarters, that being the best term I can think of, must have run those used by explorers in darkest Africa a close second. Anyone, who reminds me of our reputation as Brylcreem boys, had best think again.

At a very early hour, yet still feeling as though fresh from a steam bath, we completed our flight plan, hastened to our refuelled aeroplane, saw our passengers safely on, and then after what seemed an endless take off run, clawed our way slowly up into the air.

Strange to relate, the surface temperatures in the Gulf, sometimes dropped significantly at night and one could find on such occasions, that, in the initial stages of climb, the temperature rose, a situation known as an inversion.

The route from Bahrein to Karachi was practically due east, flying initially over the Gulf until reaching the Sharjah Peninsula, where the ground rose rapidly from the sandy shoreline to rugged mountain peaks which cut at right angles across our track and often posed weather problems.

Moist air at medium altitude would lead to the build up of thunderstorm activity over the peninsula, making the crossing rather hazardous at times. Once over, our track ran parallel to the coast of Iran and Baluchistan, just to seaward but close enough for us to appreciate just how desolate and rugged the coastal regions were. Along this coast were a number of landing strips at Jask, Gwadar and Jiwani, where in pre-war days the giant Imperial Airways land-planes used to refuel on their way through to India.

Today's air traveller, sitting comfortably, at say 35,000 feet, with a 'G&T' plus in-flight entertainment, rarely glances out at the interesting sights below, but to us, at that time, everything was new.

We had never ventured that far out of the UK before, and what we now saw had only previously been read about in geography books, so there were joint interests, navigational and general.

Stunned by the harshness of the land to our left, I sat with a somewhat dated map, checking point after point as we moved on until, the all powerful radio beacon sited at Karachi signified "I'm dead ahead, come on in".

The RAF aerodrome, which had been active for many years, was at Mauripur, a short distance outside the city, but the accommodation was very primitive. Once again we slept in tents, which was tolerable, but the toilet facilities hardly deserved that name. When the 'call' came, I was directed to a canvas-screened square with a small entrance gap in one side. I didn't expect much, because the stench prior to entry almost gave the game away. A deep pit, with a wooden rail at the top, upon which the occupiers sat with their rear ends over the pit, reading whatever was to hand, while waiting for nature to take its course. The regulars were quite used to this and sat chatting, quite unconcernedly, about things in general, but for me, that sight alone was too much. I retreated and headed for one of the few permanent buildings which had an adjoining loo, and that was that.

We were taken in to the city by service transport on our one free day, to find the same mix as in most eastern cities. One street set-aside for ladies of easy virtue, plenty of bazaar style shops, cattle wandering everywhere at will, and above it all, the buzzards scavenging anything edible in sight. They did of course inhabit the so-called "towers of silence" where the dead were placed for the buzzards to do their worst.

There was always a popular purchase at most overseas towns, and in Karachi it was carpets and tea. The standard carpet was twelve by nine feet, and I took many of these home in the months ahead, to fit into what was to be our home, and most welcome they were when so much was rationed in the UK. Tea was sold in one pound boxes, and it wasn't long before the wide boys found an outlet for these in Cairo on our return journeys, and a new racket was born. The only other items worthy of purchase were beautiful articles, often badges, made from silver and gold wire and finally, ladies shoes, which if one took along a UK style pattern, could be knocked up to order in less than a day.

I did notice how smart the Indian Service personnel and police were, mainly because of their clean, beautifully starched uniforms and their apparent high standard of discipline. It was here that we got our first taste of the Dobhi wallahs, who would launder ones clothes to perfection, "bashing" them out against local rocks we were told, and whether true or not, the end product was far superior to the limp end products elsewhere on our routes.

In due course we moved off, heading for Bangalore in central southern India, with a call at Bombay on the way. All I recall of Bombay in those early days was the large volume of shipping standing off the port, the crowded streets as we approached to land, but surprisingly enough before that, the masses of people on the beaches. I suppose the coastal spots were a break from the city, but came the Southwest monsoon, and then it was nothing but rain for months on end.

The flight on south followed the coast in the main, and to one used only to blackouts, enemy action and generally drab conditions back home, I was almost mesmerised by the sight of long stretches of bright sandy beach, fringed with palms, and an occasional small village with boats beached alongside. The war had, of course, reached India, but not yet in these remote sites. We moved slowly along until, somewhere in the region of the Portuguese settlement of Goa, we headed inland and duly settled down at the airfield of Yellahanka. There was not a lot on offer at Bangalore, but we did visit the town and I still have a menu from Winstons Bar, which has a comprehensive list of food and drink.

A short night stop and then the quick flight to Colombo, where the RAF had two aerodromes, one at Negombo and the other at Ratmalana, both quite close to the city.

There was plenty of service activity in this part of the globe as the headquarters of South East Asia Command, based at Delhi, was also operating at Kandy, a delightful spot in the central hills of Ceylon.

Again, smooth palm fringed sandy beaches where, if one could find the time, swimming and surfing were a much-appreciated bonus.

There is little else that registered at that time other than much greenery, elephants galore and ageing buildings, presumably built by early Europeans in Victorian times, or so it seemed.

The return flight home was a reversal of the outbound, except that, since we were now heading into prevailing westerly winds, it took a lot longer.

During my absence, but with my blessing and appreciation, the family had been making preparations for the forthcoming wedding, and shortly after my arrival, and with a long leave pass in my hand, the deed was done!

On June 3rd 1944, at All Saints Church, Orpington, the knot was tied in the presence of a thoroughly mixed bunch of witnesses for, almost inevitably, things went wrong.

Bob had marshalled my crew together and they turned up to ensure that there was no retreat. However, the best man, my future brother in law, who was serving with the Navy, had his leave cancelled. A quick decision was made that the first male member of the family to appear would immediately be co-opted. This proved to be a long forgotten uncle who, once the situation had been explained, stepped in and performed like a trouper. Then, my wife to be's father, a lovely old country lad from Suffolk, decided that he wasn't going to wear a tie. More consultations, but we won the day thanks to Taylor Walker's brewery. The old chap's favourite brew was an ale known as Main Line, and he was told quite positively, no tie, no beer, and that did the trick. Messages arrived stating that a number of guests could not make it and as the catering had been arranged, a group of us toured Orpington High Street, and any service personnel in uniform, male or female, found themselves invited to a first class meal. Believe it or not all then went well, and so in spite of Murphy's law, it was a successful day, in every respect.

I'd love to say that we set off for a romantic honeymoon at some exotic spot, but of course the UK was under siege and so we travelled a few miles to my sister in law's house at Forest Hill, in south London, which she had turned over to us for a few days. Murphy's Law again, for three days later there was a general recall, as the Normandy landings were just about to get under way. Don't talk to me about hard times today, and yet, even then, in spite of all, we still saw the amusing side of things, said very fond farewells, and departed for our respective units.

One thing, which my wife and I had agreed upon, was that we wished to start a family, which, although not the true reason, would ensure her discharge from the WAAF.

On arrival back at Lyneham, our crew was rapidly despatched to Karachi, and on our return I became involved in a crash, of a most particular kind.

It had been our custom to borrow service bicycles and travel in a small group to one of the local pubs, situated in the valley below Lyneham. Returning one evening, somewhat the worse for wear, our group began a series of mock attacks on each other weaving and charging all over the road when one of my attackers struck me hard on the beam, putting me and my vehicle into a ditch. To my surprise, as I tried to raise myself up, my left arm would not function, and I called out, somewhat alarmed, to my colleagues. I should have known better for there was no help and no sympathy, only shouts of "get up you silly sod!". After a few minutes, it finally sank into one chap's befuddled brain that all was not well and they all returned to help me out. Assisted by a couple of them, while a third trundled the damaged bike along, we made our way up the hill to the camp, and directly to sick quarters. Here, the MO's first question was, "have you been drinking". Swaying gently, a radio man, one Paddy Fahy, assured him that we'd had just a glass or two. I suppose the Doc had an element of sympathy, for he said no more, but settling me on to a couch he prepared to knock me out with Ether or whatever was used in those days, while he took a look at the damage which seemed to be centred in my left shoulder. I faded away, but came to very soon after to see the MO with his foot in my shoulder, or so it seemed, trying to put a dislocated shoulder back into place. That was bad enough but was not helped by the fact that the mob were still around watching the proceedings. Anyway, it was all rather painful, and I was carted off to the nearby hospital at RAF Wroughton where, next day, it was determined that more importantly than the dislocated shoulder, the circumflex nerve had been severed, resulting in a partial paralysis of my arm. I was immediately encased in a body plaster, which stretched from waist to neck, with the left arm set in a vertical position, both unsightly and uncomfortable. I often wonder if it was the brutal treatment following that incident which led to this follow up, but I'll never know. What I do know is that to this day, I have never recovered any more than a limited use of my left arm.

I was sent home on leave, and in spite of my attempts to explain what had happened, my family, friends and neighbours, were all convinced that I was a hero, a brave lad who had probably crashed, but was too modest to say so. What could one do, I just gave up and wallowed in the admiration which followed.

I stayed in plaster for some time, but eventually, and in an attempt to regain mobility, I was sent to the RAF Rehabilitation Unit at Loughborough, where the RAF had taken over the college and staffed it with many notables from the sporting world to act as Physical Training Instructors. They included Dan Maskell, Raich Carter and many other personalities who all worked hard to see us restored to good health again.

It was here that an amusing, yet embarrassing, event occurred. A York aircraft, setting off on a tour of overseas units, with many high ranking officers on board, crashed at the end of the first stage, on to the runway at Gibraltar. The passengers all suffered spinal injuries and finished up at Loughborough too. One of them, an Air Vice Marshal who had responsibility for Lyneham, heard that four members of that unit were undergoing treatment and he decided to do the decent thing for his boys and invite them along for drinks one evening. It all went well until he asked us how we had been injured, assuming I suppose that we too were survivors of aircraft accidents. I batted first, and explained in brief, the bicycle incident, number two related how he had injured his back playing rugby, which left the AVM looking a little disappointed. Number three had apparently damaged his knee playing soccer, but number four really put paid to the evening when he endeavoured to justify falling off a first floor balcony at a Nottingham hotel, when under the influence, with resultant injuries. We knew the full stories, and there is little doubt that the AVM quickly saw through the greatly modified versions we told to him. Needless to say, the evening was not a success and we were not invited again.

We always exercised in teams and in my group we had the great Hector Bolitho, who in spite of his standing in society, delighted in being one of the lads. The leading light in repair work was Nicky Zinoviev (I may well have misspelled his name), but he had great sympathy for us all, regardless, as did his assistant Pat. Poor Pat, we made her life hell.

Lost muscle control was revived in those days by a machine, which, through strategically placed pads, delivered a small electric current thereby activating wasting muscle.

In the event that a new boy arrived for treatment, Pat would hitch him up but as soon as her back was turned, we would turn the current control to it's maximum value, so that as soon as poor Pat switched on, the invalid nearly hit the roof under the influence of whatever maximum power was available.

The local residents were extremely kind to us and many were the invitations to substantial evening meals. Pubs abounded in the town and the lads made sure that they were well patronised. There were frequent telephone calls asking if someone could call and pick up walking sticks or crutches, which had been left behind the night before. The demon drink obviously had a good effect on recovery.

All good things come to an end and – too soon for my liking – I was passed as medically fit to fly and returned to 511 Squadron. During my spell away, the squadron had received it's first York aircraft, and I was advised that I would form part of one of the crews about to be appointed.

Before that, and in the short break which ensued, I was sent to RAF Llandow in South Wales, to attend a night vision course. This seemed odd since most of us had spent countless hours flying at night without problems. I guess that someone in authority had hit upon a new idea, for improved vision, although we saw no evidence of it during the short course. This was after the 'carrot theory' days. Two of us were sent off to Wales, but on arrival found that most of the chaps on the course had the same attitude. So resigned to orders we made the best of it, even to the sessions where we sat in goggles in order to become night acclimatised, prior to carrying out chosen exercises in class. In truth, we couldn't get away fast enough at the end of the day, when collectively we would head for Bridgend or Maesteg to drown our sorrows. We saw it through to the bitter end but our last night, spent in the mess, although preceded by a drinking bout in town, was little short of a disgrace. It started with the customary game of removing shoes and socks, blacking the feet with soot from the fireplace, and then, held aloft by others, placing footmarks across the ceiling. That done, accompanied by a piano-playing colleague, we broke into a war dance to the tune of Zulu Warrior, while, for reasons unknown, one guy set fire to the war maps on the wall. Alarm bells began to flash and, diplomatically, but drunkenly, I sloped off to bed.

The CO was onto it very quickly, and together with others I was summoned to his office next morning. I went in alone, and before I could even offer my apologies he said, "Woods, I understand that you were involved in the wilful destruction of my mess last night. Can you please explain why?"

I couldn't, of course, because talking of winding down just wasn't on, yet I feel that he knew this to be so, but could not afford to acknowledge it. The outcome was a stiff reprimand, but with not a word on my service record, and the others were treated likewise.

I couldn't get back to Lyneham fast enough, where I learned immediately that I was to join a Flight Lieutenant Frank Dewell, and his crew, all of whom were well decorated Bomber Command veterans. Although I didn't know it at the time, I was to see my time out with Frank until I was finally demobbed. A surprising, but very pleasant event, was the arrival of an Air Ministry Postagram stating that we had been appointed as the "Chiefs of Staff" crew. This of course meant a whole string of VIP flights, for which purpose they added a steward to our crew, the first ever to be appointed in the RAF.

I won't pretend that life became easy thereafter, on the contrary, but we became something rather special. On call at very short notice to go virtually anywhere at any time. In addition we were issued with one piece white flying suits which set us apart and made us very proud little airmen.

I spent the remainder of my flying with the RAF, in what then became known as 1359 VIP Flight, an off shoot of a similar unit based at Hendon, the latter dealing with short range flights as 24 Squadron, while we covered the long distance requirements.

Because the months, which followed, were full of variety and important personalities, I will devote the last chapter of this book to those events.

I should add that one York in particular, registered as LV633, had been fitted out as Sir Winston Churchill's personal aircraft, with a bedroom, small conference room, and other appropriate fittings, and it was our good fortune to fly this machine whenever we carried a VIP, always with Sir Winston's approval, of course. We almost carried him once too.

CHAPTER 15

A Nice Way to Prepare
for Signing Off

Although we worked extremely hard in the period which followed our appointment, we never lost sight of the fact that others had a far tougher time, engaged in operations in the closing stages of the war in Europe. Not only did we have the bonus of visiting places far removed from the war zone, but, thanks to the standing of our passengers, we were occasionally accommodated in hotels, something almost unheard of in those days and in general handling terms, almost received VIP treatment ourselves.

Before settling down to the main task, we were given a couple of 'odd jobs'. One was to take the 'Churchill' York up to Radlett and undertake a low-level fly past, followed by a static display, which together with many other aircraft types, had been set up to let a group of UNO representatives, destined to form what eventually became ICAO (The International Civil Aviation Organisation) see how aviation was developing in the UK. We saw several new military types currently under development and had a chance to chat to the brave souls who were undertaking the development and proving flights, a hairy existence.

The other was quite different. We were sent off to Cairo and ordered to fly to and fro, along the Egyptian coast to carry out icing tests on the Merlin engines. Now these engines were well proven, having been in use in a whole variety of aeroplanes for many years, so the experiment seemed a little unnecessary. However, ours was not to question why but just to obey.

A large drum of water was placed inside the aeroplane and a flexible tube led from this straight to the intake of the starboard inner engine.

Connected to this line was a hand pump, and armed with this Heath Robinson gear, the experiment commenced.

Under Frank's direction, we took it in turns to pump gallons of water straight into the intake to await results. It had long been known that engine icing could occur at temperatures well above freezing since carburettor functioning produced a temperature drop within. For normal flying, various heating devices had been designed to overcome this problem, so why our experiment? It didn't much matter because the end result was simply some extremely rough running but not much else. We conscientiously discharged our duty and reported all the visible and audible results and then returned to Lyneham. What was it all about?

We never did discover, and certainly we saw no engine modifications thereafter but doubtless there is still an appropriate file held in records somewhere.

We appreciated very early on, just what a great aeroplane the York was, being powerful, roomy, but oh so noisy! From my point of view, I had the luxury of a raised navigation position behind the co-pilot, with all necessary instruments close at hand and, most importantly, some of the new radar equipment previously used exclusively by operational commands had now been fitted to our aircraft. This proved very useful when flying over the Continent, but sadly coverage did not extend further.

Our first formal task was to pick up the Governor of Gibraltar at Northolt and return him to the Rock, arriving back at Lyneham just in time to take the Under Secretary of State for Foreign Affairs to Athens for a conference, and to follow this up with returning to deliver a group of UNO officials to Athens to join him. So the game was on, but how different life now became.

Next came a 'long one' – the Labour Government Foreign Secretary, I think his name was Hall, was desirous of visiting our various Colonies in West Africa and who better to transport him than us.

Picking him up at Northolt we departed south, calling in to the American base at Port Lyautey in order to refuel. Our first visit was to be to Bathurst, in Gambia, and the track took us over completely new and interesting territory, following the coasts of Morocco, and then French and Spanish West Africa. A short stop over and then we added the Governor of Gambia to our party and headed for Accra, on the Gold Coast (Now Ghana). Dropping our VIPs, we flew on to Lagos (Nigeria) and uplifted the Governor there, bringing him back to Accra, for a joint conference.

I found this part of the world most intriguing, for post war development lay well ahead and the west coast was still regarded as 'the white man's grave'. The RAF did have a major airfield down there at Takoradi which was set up as a jumping off point for aircraft destined to make the long flight across the desert via Nigeria, Tchad and the Sudan and on up to the Canal Zone in Egypt. Many of these aircraft were taken down to West Africa in crates on the early aircraft carriers, assembled on the way, and then flown off. History has shown what a useful lifeline this became.

On our return, we undertook two consecutive flights, which were most rewarding. The first from Northolt was, we were told, to transport some Arabian officials to Cairo, and since we did not use the VIP York, it was assumed that they were persons of minor importance.

What did seem strange, although our passengers were all in long flowing white robes, was that they grouped themselves almost presidential style, around an extremely tall figure in the centre. As they approached the aircraft the stately figure with handsome aquiline features gave the game away. Hardly a minor figure, for it was Emir Faisal, son of King Saud, leader of Saudi Arabia. This being a standard aircraft, our passengers sat in normal banked seats, and for the long haul of over eleven hours I noticed that, each time I went aft, the group were managing to play what I assumed to be a card game, accompanied by much shouting and occasionally one or the other, whom I took to be a loser, would dig into a pouch suspended from an ornamental belt and pass over a gold coin or two. Needless to say, they all wore magnificently engraved curved daggers at their waist. Not people to pick an argument with!

Shortly before arrival at Cairo, a huge Nubian escort, pushed open the flight deck door, and before we could protest, he produced a number of watches and, without a word, handed one to each of us. They were Omega watches, each engraved with the words "Faisal Al Saud", and to this day, my gift watch runs perfectly, although I am told that I would need a second mortgage to have any repairs carried out to it.

A little out of sequence, I must relate the tale of our next distinguished passenger. This time we were fully briefed and we had been entrusted with the task of taking King Abdullah, grandfather of the late King of Jordan, home to his new Kingdom. Up until that time Jordan had been mandated territory, ruled over by Abdullah as Emir. Following his visit to London, he was to become King and rule over Jordan, as the new Hashemite Kingdom.

I feel no shame in repeating an incident which occurred on this flight and which I have related in a book elsewhere, particularly since I made a dreadful mistake, yet was forgiven.

The first stage of our flight was to Naples, where Embassy staff turned up in force to escort the King into the city since we were well ahead of our scheduled 8am arrival at Lydda (Tel Aviv), this being before the modern day 'troubles'.

The King, looking every inch a regal old warrior, wearing the largest gold encased dagger I had ever seen, announced that he would not wish to travel to Naples, and as for his arrival, he did not anticipate any great reception at Lydda. I don't know what diplomats are supposed to do in such circumstances but I give them full marks for their efforts in attempting to convince the King that he should change his mind, though all to no avail.

Frank spoke to his aide and it was agreed that it was better to get under way, rather than let the King sit things out on a smelly old York.

So the embassy team departed, and so did we, with the King still sitting bolt upright in his seat... what a wonderful old man.

Our delaying tactics to ensure arrival at the correct time had already been decided and as we approached the Egyptian coast at Mersa Matruh we put them into action, by making a turn to the north, the intention being to fly for a short while, then turn south and finally resume the correct track.

So off we headed, with twilight fast dwindling as the sun appeared above the eastern horizon. After a short while, I asked Frank to come round to the southerly heading and no sooner had we settled down than I heard a disturbance from the rear, and the flight deck door opened to allow the entry of an obviously angry aide.

It had all happened so quickly, but apparently as we headed north the King had prepared himself for morning prayers, with the sunrise on our right.

No sooner had he set about prayers than we turned so that he was then facing west. This could have led to a major international incident, maybe with the loss of our heads! However, the King, after our explanation and apologies, forgave us, indicative of the man that he was.

He still insisted that there would be no major reception, but in the circuit at Lydda, we could see masses of people in and around the airfield. It was all so memorable, for as we taxied in we saw rank upon rank of uniformed members of the Arab Legion. Doors were opened and the military band struck up, but then the crowd broke through to hail the King. One had to be impressed by their enthusiasm and in truth it was very emotional to see the high esteem in which they held their leader. Before we left the flight deck, an English-speaking Aide came up and presented each of us with a gold watch. One never refused a gift under such circumstances as it was better than having one's head lopped off for our (my) sin. Needless to say, I never did live down this event and it still makes a good, and true, anecdote.

Not too many years ago, I attended a Trophies and Awards banquet laid on by my Livery Company, The Honourable

Company of Air Pilots and Air Navigators, and the then King of Jordan, King Hussein, who was the guest of honour, was both amused and delighted to hear the tale of that epic flight. There is no point in boring readers with a catalogue of our many flights, which followed, except to mention one more. We were sent to Northolt to pick up some unspecified freight, which we were to take to Prague. I noticed that the large boxes, which were being onloaded, were all moved under an armed guard. It wasn't until we were airborne, that Frank, who was already in the picture, told us that we were delivering the new post war Czech currency – all of it! I suppose if we had headed for some far away remote spot we could have made a fortune for ourselves, but then again that was a crazy notion. It was interesting to visit a recently occupied country for the first time and to see these fine people struggling to return to some sort of normality. Believe it or not, they even managed to find a nightclub for us to visit.

While all of this was going on, the efforts of our wonderful forces in Europe had brought the war to a successful conclusion and the RAF, in spite of events in the far east were looking further into the future, as indeed we all were. I therefore applied for a permanent commission, realising that as a married man, with responsibilities, which included our first child, we would, to put it bluntly, need the money, which as I had now attained the rank of Flight Lieutenant, was not to be sneezed at.

The RAF, playing safe, offered most of my kind an extended service commission, to be reviewed in six months, but with civil flying on the increase, it seemed better to head that way if possible.

Life at Lyneham became very relaxed, as evinced by some of the off duty antics. I recall one memorable mess party, which concluded with an attempt to bring a Baby Austin car into the mess. Getting it through the main doors was no problem, but beyond that it looked as if the bar doors would have to come off. No less a person than the Padre saved the day and talked us out of the final stages. There was also great excitement when flight commanders Stafford Bull terrier was found wandering the camp with yellow and red bands painted around his vast stomach. All rather silly now, but reflecting upon such events it is as well to remember that most of our crews had had a rough time in Bomber Command, and with a final end to all hostilities in sight, a slow steady wind-down was more than justified.

Our small unit, 1359 Flight was moved to Bassingbourne in Cambridgeshire, where we saw our time out until demobilisation.

It was at this time that what was to have been a proud moment for our crew, fell flat due to circumstances beyond our control. We were ordered to take the VIP York to Northolt, post haste, in order to rush Sir Winston Churchill off to Paris for a top level meeting. Arriving at Northolt full of enthusiasm, we were greeted with the news that a strong crosswind at Orly would not permit us to land and it had been decided to use the King's Dakota instead. What a horrible disappointment for us. We did however get to see the great man since we had been invited to lunch at the mess where he too was to dine. I'll not forget his entrance. Seemingly a huge figure, rosy cheeks wreathed in smiles, he marched in with his minions, nodding and smiling at all present, obviously out to enjoy himself. At the top table, we saw ample evidence of his liking for a certain liquid refreshment, which seemed to enhance that wonderful aura which surrounded him at all times. All too soon he was on his way, and so passed the day when we nearly had the honour of transporting our great wartime leader to foreign parts. There was plenty of spare time, a good deal of which I spent motoring around the aerodrome perimeter in a colleague's old Ford, with no one questioning where we were able to find the petrol, aiming an equally aged 4/10 shot gun at almost anything which moved, although there were plenty of hares on such sites.

When " Victory in Europe" was announced, it was our good fortune to be on the island of Malta for the celebrations of VE day. It surely requires little imagination, considering how they had suffered and survived, to hear that everyone went wild. I remember that, although we obviously took on a good load of alcohol, we sat back mesmerised while it seemed that the Navy fired off all their remaining ammunition and flares, over Grand Harbour, a marvellous sight to behold.

Not too long afterwards, a friend who always seemed to be one jump ahead of me, telephoned to say that BOAC were recruiting navigators and that he had already signed up. He suggested that it might be a good idea to jump on the bandwagon as soon as possible. I needed no pushing and rapidly submitted my most useful recent flying experience to them. I was accepted – and there I stayed for the next 18 happy years.

In due course I went through the usual demob procedures at that most dismal of all places, Uxbridge, and with my pork pie hat, striped grey suit, black brogues and herringbone Raglan overcoat, sadly waved goodbye to the RAF.

So what did I gain and learn in those seven years?

A profession of course, because although that was not the intention, it was the end product and led me on to a working life in aviation.

All the seminars, lectures and philosophical books in the world could not have given me the education in human nature that I took away with me.

Then there was the comradeship, which still lives on, born of sacrifice, one for another and bravery beyond belief from youngsters not long out of school. So many paid the ultimate price and sacrificed their young lives to see our country oppose Nazi domination – and bless them all, they succeeded.

I have never stopped believing that service discipline and our good, basic moral upbringing was the key to our success. I am sure we would all benefit if such thoughts and actions prevailed amongst the young today. Perhaps one day, who knows, things will change for the better, but until then, my friends and I have something rather special to hold on to and no one can take it away.

I feel certain that the epilogue which follows will sum up the thoughts of those who were fortunate enough to survive to be present on that memorable day which I shall attempt to describe.

EPILOGUE

A Fitting Memorial

Towards the end of the war, two of the No.5 Group Squadrons, my own, No.61, together with No.50 moved to an airfield at Skellingthorpe, a site that was pretty well on the boundary of the City of Lincoln. Both squadrons had been in the thick of things right up until hostilities ceased, and both suffered very high loss rates.

A group of survivors decided that a suitable memorial should be constructed and as part of the preliminary work formed a memorial association and invited past squadron members to join and subscribe. The venture was a great success, culminating in the erection of a beautiful green marble obelisk, with, amongst other things, the squadron crests engraved on one side. The site provide by the local council was on the spot where, many years before, one of the runway thresholds had stood, the whole area now being a housing estate.

June 3rd 1989 was the appointed day for the dedication and unveiling, oddly enough, our wedding anniversary.

I think that most of us who made the journey north were totally overwhelmed by the end product of all the planning and by the number of folk present. Old crew members came from Australia, New Zealand, South Africa, Canada and even the USA, to be joined by widows, wives, friends and relatives, for all of whom this would prove to be a memorable day.

The local street was crowded as the RAF Band from Cranwell marched in to provide the music for a very moving service. The Bishop of Lincoln conducted the formal ceremony and dedication, during which he preached about the horrors and penalties of war. Genuine though his thoughts may have been, I'm afraid they were not really taken on board by the assembled throng who had come to honour lost comrades who paid the ultimate price, thereby allowing the Bishop and others to be present.

During the service the hymns were sung with great feeling and gusto by aircrew who were not usually regarded as being in any way emotional – but this was something special. I know that I was in the company of many hundreds, who behaved in like manner, when I shed more than a tear or two.

The unveiling was carried out by Marshal of the Royal Air Force, Sir Michael Beetham, who had in fact served on one of the squadrons as a Flight Lieutenant during the closing stages of operations.

Sir Michael spoke our language when he referred to the terrible losses suffered by both squadrons, recalling two VCs – Flt/Lt Bill Reid RAFVR of No.61 Squadron (who was present) and Flying Officer Leslie Manser RAFVR of No 50 Squadron, after whom the local children's school was named. He went on to remind us of how the good folk of the City of Lincoln had heard the bombers making their way out, night after night, and returning in the early hours of the morning. He added, a little cynically, that there were no complaints about aircraft noise in those days. (I must digress and add that in none of the many stations and counties in which I was based did I ever find anything to compare with the welcome and appreciation shown to us by the good folk of Lincoln who truly took us to their hearts, and indeed still do.)

At the conclusion of the Service, families and friends laid wreaths as did many local youngsters, another moving part of the day. Then came the most significant time of all for we survivors. The official groups formed up some distance along the road, with the RAF band at their head, ready for the march past, while we veterans were shepherded into a side road, all part of a pre-arranged plan as yet undisclosed to us.

A Drill Sergeant, obviously a long-service one at that, addressed us thus: "Right! Come on you 'orrible lot! Form yourselves into three flights and we'll show these young buggers just what marching is all about!"

In the normal course of events such an order would have been wasted on aircrew, or at best would have attracted shouts of derision, but today was different. The band struck up and led the parade past the saluting base, the first contingent being trainee officer cadets from Cranwell, the RAF's future pilots, followed by airmen from a local base, Reservists, the Royal Observer Corps and – bless 'em – the Air Training Corps, all tremendously smart.

Under the orders of 'our' NCO we moved out behind the column with one thought in mind. We were here to honour our lost friends and no one was going to outdo us. I could hardly believe the outcome. Forget Horse Guards Parade and Trooping the Colour with all its pomp and precision, forward we marched, all in step, heads held high, medals galore, as we approached the memorial to the applause of all present. It was unbelievably emotional and, as in the preceding service, I saw many a damp cheek alongside me as tears flowed. The band rose to the occasion for as the first of our flights came abeam the saluting base, they struck up with "Those magnificent men in their flying machines". I could see the look of pride on Sir Michael's face, for after all, he was one of us and it was his day too.

The occasion had been preceded by a get together party in Lincoln the night before, but Birchwood Council had thrown open their village hall to us, hence another party lay ahead, with memory after memory flowing from these fine chaps who might afterwards, never meet again.

In fact the Association do now hold an annual service at the memorial, but the attendance numbers are dwindling fast and on the most a recent occasion we were down to one flight, but they still find a band for the march past and there is always a party in Lincoln to warm things up. One lovely touch is that the local authority has promised to maintain the site in perpetuity, and on each visit I have made it is gratifying to see that they are doing just that. Even the Manser School nearby has its own collection of memorabilia provided by the lads of both squadrons and they always invite us along after the visit to meet the children, who have been taught the history of events and mark them in their own way.

The Dedication Ceremony was titled 'Operation Failed to Return' and we are all so proud to know that our lost comrades were properly honoured and will now never be forgotten. If only we could convey our sentiments to the world at large, it might just be a better place in which to live.